"I Get To"

"I *Get* To"

How Using the *Right Words* Can Radically Transform Your Life, Relationships & Business

Alicia Dunams

Download the *I Get To* Resource Guide

**The free companion items to this book,
including printable handouts and book updates
are available at:
www.AliciaDunams.com/IGetTo**

Please access these items now before you forget.

DEDICATION

To Izzy

Table of Contents

Foreword

As one of the world's foremost experts on empathic listening with a top-selling book on the subject, I was recently commissioned to teach empathy to the Russian government.

It was not the easiest job, but someone *had* to do it.

Scratch that.

It was not the easiest job, and someone *got* to do it. And that someone was me!

A few shifts in the words we use can instantly create a different outcome in our life, relationships, and work.

Language

Throughout time, space, and culture, language spans the history of thought from the archaic, such as the ancient Greeks, to the futurists podcasting about human performance. From religion to governmental authorities to the rise of corporate cultures that dominate this era, language can be traced to the following forms:

Words.

What we say and how we say it is the foundation of how we relate to others. A simple question and the tone in which it is delivered can either compel or motivate others by activating oxytocin production and their prefrontal cortex (or intelligent brain). On the other hand, a question can trigger cortisol production (like that time your 3rd grade teacher drilled you with "What's the Capital of North Dakota?) and reach deep into the well of the limbic system, that reptilian sector of the brain that screams fight/flight/freeze. With that, the intention behind your questions and the tone in which you deliver can make or break your relationships.

Tone.

The tone you use is as important as the words you say. You want to be mindful that you are talking *with* the other person, as opposed to *over* them, *at* them, or *to* them. Deliver words with a tone that invites people into the conversation with you.

Non-verbal.

A simple pause, three seconds or more, can support you in turning a rash reaction into a thoughtful response. Simply put, non-verbal communication is as important as the words we use. So, shut up for a minute and just listen. Remember that poise – a quality in short supply – begins with a pause. It could even save a life.

Crafting our daily language with effective words and tone is a true art. Alicia Dunams and her book and movement, *I Get To,* is a gift to connect you to this craft with the sentence starters and communication skills to be successful in life.

Because *I Get To. You Get To. We Get To.*

Dr. Mark Goulston, Author of *Just Listen: Discover the Secret to Getting Through to Absolutely Anyone*

"The danger is that it's just talk. Then again, the danger is that it's not. I believe you can speak things into existence."

—Jay Z

Introduction

Don't be dismayed by the gap; be inspired by the gap.

Alicia Dunams

I'm fascinated with gaps—the space between where you are and where you want to be. I tell my students to not be dismayed by the gap, but instead fall in love with the gap. For within the gap lies innovation, growth, and opportunity.

CEOs of every corporation, for instance, wake in the morning thinking of the gap and strategies to close the gap. Everyone from science journalists to Navy Seals to executives have learned how to deep-dive into their thinking, processes, and begin to close this distance in the pursuit of peak performance. The gap, therefore, is an exciting place to be.

You may ask, "*What do gaps have to do with this book?*"

To that end, it takes certain skill sets to bridge the gap. Emotional intelligence is one skill. Technical skills are another. Communication . . . meaning the words, intonation, and non-verbal cues we use . . . is another.

That is where this book comes in. It will cover:

How using the *right words* will radically transform your life, relationships, and business.

One gap I have seen in people, after countless hours facilitating trainings for entrepreneurs and corporations alike, is a fear of speaking up and using their voice, not knowing what to say, or saying the *wrong words*.

Words like:

"I'm trying to mentor students on overcoming mental blocks, but the school won't compensate me for my time."

"No, I haven't finished my book, because I have to focus on my business."

"I can't afford that."

"I'm disappointed because they didn't get back to me. It's bad customer service. I'm going to write a negative Yelp review."

These are examples of negative language patterns. They seem like innocuous and rational statements. Words like these unconsciously slip from our mouth . . . either from time to time or on a daily basis. Such word choices are the verbal manifestation of what is going on in our subconscious mind. Yet, these words, given how they connect to the science of our internal belief systems, can both disempower and sabotage our success.

Let's radically transform these samples:

"I'm mentoring students on overcoming mental blocks, and I'm committed to enrolling the school to compensate me for my time."

"Yes, I'm working on my book and committed to being finished by May 1. It's rewarding, as I get to work on my business at the same time."

"I choose not to purchase that service at this time."

"I'm waiting to hear back. In the meantime, I've scheduled a time this Friday to meet with the customer service department to provide feedback on what is working and not working."

Simple reframes, yes. I worked hard to get here. However, I wasn't always so aware.

In 2013, my friend Lewis Howes enrolled me in a 5-day immersion transformational training. Because Lewis is kind of a big deal, it was an instant "yes."

At that time, my life looked like a dream from the outside looking in. I was engaged to a business executive who loved me to the moon; we lived in affluent Marin County in a beautiful home. My business was consistent and turnkey, giving me the ability to work less than 20 hours a week and travel internationally several times a year.

But underneath it all, I lacked joy. I was disconnected. I was taking life for granted.

During this particular training, I was introduced to a new way of being and speaking. My life was about to change forever.

Dream it. Declare it. Deliver it.

From a very early age, I knew the power of words. In middle school, I wrote my first bucket list. This is the definition of intentional: write a list of things you want to do before you die, and then go do them. The list included snorkeling the Great Barrier Reef in Australia, trekking the Himalayas, and backpacking around the world. I wrote my bucket list at age 12. By the age of 22, I had done all three . . . and graduated from UCLA.

Yet, this is not a book about bucket lists. This is a book about intentional communication.

Communication is the exchange of information or ideas between two or more parties. (Even though I do believe self-communication and affirmations are important for shifting your mindset, those topics are addressed in Chapter 3 and 12.)

My bucket list was not a communication tool with others. It was all about me. There was little to no negotiation, enrollment, collaboration, connection, or intimacy with others.

In fact, to the contrary.

My mom and dad said I could only go on my around-the-world trip if I traveled with a friend. I agreed. As a graduation present from UCLA, they paid for my trip. However, a few months before the trip, my friend canceled. I lied to my parents and went anyway. I didn't tell my parents the truth until several weeks later. Even then, my way of communicating with them was through a letter, as I was too scared to tell them over the phone.

I share this story to show I wasn't mature enough, or courageous enough, to handle the difficult discussions that happen with others when it comes to navigating the complexities of important communication.

Why did I write this book?

For over two decades, I have been a communications professional, focusing on distilling diverse and complex content into a concise message. My first business, after an exciting few years of traveling around the world twice and living a life as a travel writer and photographer, was in technical documentation. I wrote content without emotion or frivolity—the how-tos, standard operating procedures, and technical reports for many software, financial services, and bio-pharmaceutical companies.

I went on to write a self-help book and host conferences for women and eventually create the business I have today, which supports people in writing books.

I studied and trained as a leadership trainer focused on emotional intelligence, communication tools, and diversity issues. My desire to write this book comes from seeing how people struggle to use their voice or find the right words.

Foundations of the practice

This book will help you choose and use the right words as well as manage the energy beneath the words you use. What's happening on the inside is most often expressed in our attitudes and comes to the surface to reflect our true beliefs. For example, you can declare the affirmative "I am joyful," but actually be seething on the inside. In this case, there's an energetic misalignment or contradiction.

You want to be aware of how your external words and tone mirror your internal frequency. Simply put, mantras don't work if the energy underneath does not match the mantra.

If your energetic tone is disempowered, exudes any contradictions, or steers your way of thinking and feeling toward "I don't believe what I am saying," then deeper work must be done.

This brings up my next point. In life, we have a tool kit. The 40 communication starters set forth in this book are only one part of the tool kit.

My recommendation is to learn and implement the following three foundational practices, which are essential elements of the communication tool kit.

Three essential practices

1) **Gratitude.** Being grateful is a great stabilizer. You instantly become happier because you are focused on being grateful for right-now realities versus future expectations. In the article, "Neuroscience Reveals How Gratitude Literally Changes Your Brain to be Happier," by The Power of Ideas, ideapod.com, Jan. 17, 2017, https://ideapod.com/neuroscience-reveals-gratitude-literally-changes-brain-happier/, UCLA's Mindfulness Awareness Research Center says that "regularly expressing gratitude changes the molecular structure of the brain, keeps the gray matter functioning, and makes us

healthier and happier." Gratitude calms the central nervous system and makes you less reactive. To that end, grateful people have more happiness and peace.

Tool: Create a daily practice of writing or declaring five things you are grateful for.

2) **Breathe.** Breathing can be our saving grace. It can be as simple as taking a three-second pause or three breaths in and out to shift from a rash reaction to a deliberative response. Meditation, the practice of achieving a mentally clear and emotionally calm state, includes focusing on the breath. Spending at least 10 minutes a day in a meditative state, eyes closed, and focused on your breath or sounds in nature, is a game changer. Conscious breathing supports our word usage and delivery. It gives us pause as we shift moment to moment in our daily comings and goings.

Tool: Start a daily 10-minute meditation practice.

3) **Awareness.** Awareness is the state of being conscious about something. Awareness is being open and vulnerable to the process of relating to others. Awareness is also understanding your "come from" or "way of being" and how and why you are responding a certain way. This leads us to our awareness of the Three Essential Responses.

Three essential responses

Marla N. Mattenson, M.A., Relationship and Communications Expert (www. marlamattenson.com), states:

"We all have Three Essential Responses, which are equally important in the process of creating a life you love. Each of the three types of responses arises to give you the opportunity to see your blind spots more clearly and to live in a fully aligned and integrated way." Mattenson describes each one as follows.

1) The Automatic Response

The Automatic Response is your first, unscripted, internal reaction to an event, situation, or thought. This is the default—the emotional response that you don't have control over. Stress, conflict, praise, or anything uncomfortable can set off the automatic response. Without awareness, this response will lead directly into words spoken aloud that you immediately regret saying. Later, you may think, "Why did I say that?" "Why did I lie?" or "Why didn't I just say nothing or thank you?"

Let's make something clear: Automatic Responses are not intentionally inauthentic or disingenuous. They come from a pre-programmed response system in your brain that you don't have control over. And yet, others can feel the mismatch between what you're saying out loud and what you're feeling inside when you give voice to the Automatic Response.

For example, you attend a 20-year high school reunion looking fit and better than you did when you were a teenager. You bump into your old friend, and, let's say, time was not so good to her.

She says "Sue, WOW you look amazing, better than you did at junior prom!"

And out pops the meaningless flattery. "Oh my gosh, Pam. You look great, too!"

This was an Automatic Response.

Your awareness after the fact is guiding you to take a different approach the next time you feel the need to give a compliment for a compliment.

To transform the Automatic Response and set yourself up for the next time you receive a compliment, imagine a similar scenario and this time, you intentionally pause, feel the truth of the compliment, and allow yourself to receive, "[Pause] I receive that. Thank you!"

2) The Intellectual Response

The Intellectual Response implies you intellectually understand and want to believe what you are saying; yet the underlying energy is misaligned because you don't actually believe the words.

The Intellectual Response, for example, is in play when we read a book and share the information as our own when we haven't experienced it yet. You have to use your own imagination to connect with the truth of what you're saying. Again, this is an important step in awareness and integration.

For example, you say the mantra, "Money comes to me easily, frequently, and consistently." At the same time, you are thinking about all of your unpaid bills and the recent round of job cuts at work. You have financial stress to the max, yet you forcefully continue to say the mantra, "Money comes to me easily, frequently, and consistently." You intellectually believe money comes easily and frequently (as there has been evidence of it in the past), or you've witnessed others experiencing it, yet you don't believe it's true for you because you're in a financial quagmire that's causing you daily duress. Your words and your beliefs don't match.

In this case, Mattenson states, "Your belief does not align with the meaning behind your words." In other words, "You don't believe what you're saying because it's not in your experience."

The Intellectual Response is an important phase in the journey of creating the life you love. When we use our imagination to visualize our desires for the future, we must first intellectually understand *and believe* what we are creating before we manifest it. We use our imagination to feel what it will be like when we have money coming to us easily, frequently, and consistently. And the truth is that when we can imagine something in our mind and feel the universal truth of our desire, it already exists. Just not in the three-dimensional world. Our desire exists in the "Unseen World" and we must use our Intellectual Response to call into manifestation what we desire.

3) The Experiential Response

The Experiential Response is what happens after you've passed through both phases of Automatic and Intellectual Responses and had experiences that you've integrated into your life. You genuinely believe what you say because you know it's true on a cellular level. The Experiential Response is the trifecta when energy, tone, and words all align.

For example, a colleague at work needs help in their casework, and you graciously ask, "Would it be supportive if I stay after and advise you on the best strategies to move forward?"

Or to take the previous example of money manifestation, you now live life in abundance. You write a check to a charity organization, and you move in faith that your source of abundance is greater than you.

When you are naturally responding to life with the Experiential Response, you are coming from a place of service and abundance.

Keep in mind that it makes no difference if we are newer or more advanced with our communication skills—all of us will vacillate between these three responses from moment to moment.

Conflicts arise when one or more parties feel unseen or unheard. When you begin using the communication starters in this book, you want to ensure you are as present, open, and free from judgment as possible. Use this knowledge of the Three Essential Responses to become more and more aware of what you're saying, how you're saying it, and how your words are impacting your internal world as well as those around you.

Communication and neuroscience

Christine Comaford, Neuroscience-Based Leadership & Culture Coach (www.smarttribesinstitute. com), sums up nicely how understanding neuroscience is essential for developing a company culture that effectively communicates and thrives. In her article, "Hijack: How Your Brain Blocks Performance," Forbes.com, October 21, 2012, https://www. forbes. com/sites/christinecomaford/2012/10/21/hijack-how-your-brain-blocks-performance/, Comaford describes the role neuroscience in human development like this:

> "Your brain has three essential parts. The first part—the brain stem or reptilian brain—sits at the base of your skull. It's the oldest and most primitive part of the brain, and it controls

balance, temperature regulation, and breathing. It acts out of instinct and is primarily a stimulus-response machine with survival as its focus.

"Layered on top of the brainstem is the mammalian brain, which controls and expresses emotion, short-term memory, and the body's response to danger. The key player here is the limbic system, the emotional center of the brain where the fight/flight/freeze response is. Its primary focus is also survival, though it is also the seat of anger, frustration, happiness, and love.

"Let's combine the limbic system with the survival mechanism in the reptilian brain. This creates the powerful combo pack we'll call the 'critter brain,' as my mentor Carl Buchheit of NLP Marin terms it. Our critter brain doesn't care about quality of life—it cares about survival. And the key to staying alive is belonging, or being like the other critters in the environment.

"The third part of the brain is the neocortex. This part of the brain is most evolved in human beings and houses the prefrontal cortex. The prefrontal cortex enables us to plan, innovate, solve complex problems, think abstract thoughts, and have visionary ideas. It allows us to measure the quality of our experience, compare it to an abstract ideal, and yearn for change. The prefrontal cortex enables us to have advanced behaviors including tool making, language, and higher-level consciousness.

For the purposes of simplicity, we'll distill the above down to two states: the Critter State, where we don't have access to all parts of our brain and thus are reactive, are in fight/flight/freeze, or are running safety programs; and the Smart State, where we have easy access to all of our resources and can respond from choice."

Comaford, interesting to note, was a speaker at one of the women's conferences I produced, and we both worked with Carl Buchheit of NLP Marin, who she mentions in this article. When I worked with Carl, he showed me how the critter brain was running my life and sabotaging my relationships, and that my past decisions have been based on the fact that I feel "safe" when I am "unsafe." Yes, people, I am still a work in progress.

With that, let me unpack Comaford's content for you. Our critter brain is 100% focused on keeping us safe. Our interactions with other people can sometimes make us feel attacked, such as being asked a simple question in the wrong tone or receiving an out-of-context glare. Using the right words, in addition to taking a moment or breath to calm our critter brain, will help us move from constricted, critter brain thinking to more expansive Smart Brain thinking.

Can words change systems?

When I posed a question on LinkedIn about words changing social dynamics, a friend shared that she feels words are powerful in personal development but doesn't think that words can change "The System." I believe the words we use can change the system. We have already seen this happen.

The #MeToo movement, which women used to express the systemic underbelly of sexual assault and harassment, exploded when eight women, including actress Rose McGowan, garnered the courage to share their stories to *The New York Times* in a bombshell report detailing decades worth of sexual misconduct allegations against now-disgraced Hollywood mogul Harvey Weinstein. Politicians and A-List news personalities were next. Firings occurred, people took notice, and the decades-long practice of systematically sweeping these issues under the rug came to an end.

Words give you a voice and can change "The System" once words are turned into mandatory policy and procedures.

Cat got your tongue?

Sometimes we encounter circumstances where we don't know what to say or are afraid to speak. In her article, "Why We Don't Speak Up," psychologytoday.

com, February 13, 2018, https://www.psychologyto-day.com/us/blog/conversational-intelligence/201802/why-we-don-t-speak, Judith E. Glaser writes:

> "If we fear that speaking up will lead to rejection, we may give up our voice, silence our voice or speak our voice in an inauthentic way. These choices enable us to hide but with a deleterious after-effect: giving up our voice masks our true identity and diminishes our uniqueness. Hence, this decision to silence our voice leads to illness, failure, and a disempowered life."

When this is the case, the tools in this book can bridge the gap from being voiceless to using your voice.

Personally, I'm normally loud and proud, and using my voice isn't an issue. However, there have been a few times I silenced my voice because I didn't want to subvert the power dynamic. Like the time I was being interviewed by financial journalist Jean Chatzsky on radio during a book tour, and she asked me a "throw-me-under-the-bus" question. (I tell this story in detail in Chapter 29. Authors, leaders, and pundits alike must be prepared when a journalist throws a curveball. Look at it as an opportunity to reframe.)

I use my voice in my work as a facilitator and advocate. In Chapter 25, there is a script that I constructed from a LinkedIn conversation, and I personally find it of value for when boundaries have been crossed personally or professionally.

In the pages that follow, my basic advice to readers will be: **Use the *right words* and you can radically transform your life and the world.**

1
I get to vs. I have to

Perspective pivots are possible any time by anyone.

Denise Taylor

Every other week or so, I host a YouTube video series called "Go Deep: Intimate Interviews with Today's Influencers." On one episode, I interviewed my mentor and friend Chris Lee, transformational trainer and author of *Transform Your Life: 10 Principles of Abundance and Prosperity* (www. chrisleemotivator.com). In this interview, he talked about how language can create an abundant life. Specifically, he talked about shifting "I have to" to "I get to."

For example, change "I have to pick up the kids from school" to "I get to pick up the kids from school." Or, "I have to make $10,000 this month to cover all my bills" to "I get to make $10,000 this month to cover all my bills." Whenever you use the words "I have to," you cement a mindset of dread. The words "I get to" create excitement, and the perspective that it's a gift or blessing. This simple reframe can create drastic shifts in your life.

I posted this video clip on LinkedIn, and instantly received a gift that drastically changed my life. It came in the form of a comment, and is the inspiration for this book:

> "Thank you so much for the clip of Chris Lee talking about 'I get to' versus 'I have to.' I founded the nonprofit We GET To after our daughter passed away from leukemia, and we experienced the power of turning our have-to into get-tos. Her most incredible example being, "I get to have chemo," realizing not everyone has a diagnosis, hope for a cure, or means for medical care."

> "My life-changing 'get to' came completely altering my course of life. When we were about to gather with family and friends at her grave, I prayed for the 'get to' as I heard repeating in my thoughts, 'I have to bury my daughter. Please help me find the get-to.' Immediately I was given the thought, 'Only one woman in all the world got

to be Joanne's mom. She's the one who gets to release her back into heaven's loving care.' Gratitude completely dissolved the sorrow. Our story and power of 'get to' awareness is shared in the memoir *Heavenly Birth: A Mother's Journey. A Daughter's Legacy.* Perspective pivots are possible any time by anyone." (Comment from *Denise Taylor,* from *LinkedIn*).

This is a powerful way to start this book, and it's really a powerful way to view life, relationships, and business:

That you, at any moment, can shift perspective. That you, at any moment, are bigger than your circumstances.

Language is life

You can pivot perspective and change your life by simply shifting your language. The energy we breathe into the words we use begins the manifestation process and the life we want to create.

So, choose your words carefully.

I *Get* To . . . Write

During this writing exercise, change your previous "have tos" to "get tos."

For example: Change "I have to go to work" to "I get to go to work."

Why is it a "get to"? List reasons why you are grateful for this "get to."

"I have to _____ (verb +)" to

"I get to _____ (verb +)."

"I have to _____ (verb +)" to

"I get to _____ (verb +)."

"I have to _____ (verb +)" to

"I get to _____ (verb +)."

"I have to _____(verb +)" to

"I get to _____ (verb +)."

"I have to _____ (verb +)" to

"I get to _____ (verb +)."

Thoughts:

_____

_____

_____

2
Yes, if . . . vs.
No, because . . .

All our dreams can come true, if we have the
courage to pursue them.

Walt Disney

When my daughter was in middle school, she was invited to attend leadership training at Disneyland. I happily joined along as a parent chaperone. As we wandered through the miniature streets of Disneyland with our guide, the students learned a variety of leadership principles from Walt Disney and his founding team, who as a collective have shared that, when they worked with Walt Disney, you left "the room more inspired than when you came in it. [. . .] that's leadership." (Robert Niles, "Disney Legends recall Walt Disney and the 'Yes, if . . .' way of management," themeparkinsider.com, November 11, 2009, http://www.themeparkinsider. com/flume/200911/1551/).

My daughter and I discovered Walt Disney didn't like to be told, "No." Disney felt if you're going to tell someone "No," there's typically an excuse attached. For example, "No, because we are over budget" or "No, because I don't have the time." Robert Niles also writes, ". . . Walt kept employees engaged and contributing by not shooting down suggestions, but instead steering employees toward improving their ideas." So, what happens if you rephrase your "No, because" to a "Yes, if"? Instead of explaining why something cannot be done, let the other party know what it's going to take to get the job done. Coming from "Yes, if" creates possibility and opportunity. When you come from "Yes, if" you don't cut off creative energy . . . you instead create possibility and collaboration.

Lesson learned: "No" is followed by an excuse. "Yes" is followed by a possibility.

When to say "No"

There's a big conversation in the world of personal and business development to say "No" more often. When you say "No" it gives you the time to focus on what you might have said "Yes" to. Also, if you are a person who suffers from "shiny bright object" syndrome, a "No" can keep you grounded and on course. Distractions can often be dressed up as opportunities.

Let's say you're working with a business coach to turn your ice cream shop into a franchise. Then, someone approaches you to distribute your ice cream brand in stores. Feels like two different directions for a small business owner to consider, doesn't it? Well, yes and no. There is evidence that this is 100% possible, just ask Ben and Jerry. And there is evidence that focusing on one direction works too— for example my favorite ice cream brand is sold in Whole Foods and does not have storefront locations.

So how do you decide? This is when the full-bodied "Yes" comes into play . . . your "Hell, Yes!" If your lips are saying yes, and your body is saying no, it's not a full-bodied "Yes." You are on your default setting and you said "Yes" out of fear of missing out or making the wrong choice.

Cancel, cancel, and try again.

Your words must match your energetic frequency.

And, if you are in fact a full-bodied "No," honor that. If you object to something and don't want any part of it, just say, "No." Do not share excuses. Stand firm in your "No."

However, to come from a place of possibility, I always say, "Yes, if." This brilliant yet simple statement recalibrates one's mindset from the negative to the affirmative, from obstacles to opportunities.

For example:

Request: "Come and teach your course in Dubai."
Response: "Yes, if you provide 1st class round trip airfare and accommodations."

Request: "I'm going out of town for business. Can you watch my child over the weekend?"
Response: "Yes, if you pay for a babysitter on Friday night because I have plans and help clean up when you pick him up Sunday evening."

Request: "Can you loan me $1000 dollars?"
Response: "Yes, if you sign a promissory note and make your first of four payments in seven days."

And going back to our earlier example:

Request: "I'm interested in supporting you in taking your ice cream brand, which is currently in franchised storefronts, and distributing it nationwide to grocery chains."
Response: "Yes, if you write the business plan, secure $250,000 in financing to solidify the manufacturing process, and acquire a wholesale distribution deal that I can approve."

The "Yes, if" creates possibility, collaboration with others, and an opportunity to voice your requests.

Here's an example of an actual request that I said "No, because…" to:

"You have a great platform. Do you want to host your own radio show on America's Greatest Platform?"

And this is how I could have turned it into a "Yes, if . . .":

"Wow, thank you for the compliment. I have many opportunities like this come to me on a daily basis. Yes, if I receive a monthly stipend of $5k, a choice of when my radio show airs and in what markets, and a reserved parking space."

"Yes, if" is a negotiation strategy, and if your requests are a deal breaker than the other party must say "No, because" or "Yes, if" if they are truly savvy and will negotiate for what they want.

If it turns into a negotiation, it's important to note, you want to ensure you keep the tone of the conversation "firm, friendly, and fair," as noted in my clients', Lisa Leslie, former Olympian and WNBA player, and Bridgette Chambers, book, *From the Court to the Boardroom.*

Try it, you may like it

"Yes, if" is a great approach to start using if you're naturally a "no" person.

And rightly so.

In our modern era, we're inundated with a constant influx of distractions and information overload.

"No, because" has become a coping mechanism—our automatic, knee-jerk response, and default setting to shut out fear and stay safe.

Psychologists tell us that we are conditioned to say "No." The older we get, the more we say "No" in a Yes/No ratio. If it's new and different, we are conditioned to say "No" to it. A scared or confused mind says no. We are so used to saying "No," we don't even know we are saying "No."

The problem is that "No, because" doesn't work with innovation or anything creative for that matter. It doesn't foster ideas or inspire disruptive thought. It can actually nip something great in the bud before it even begins to take root.

How can you turn problems into possibilities today?

How can you turn "No, because..." to "Yes, if..."?

I *Get* To . . . Say "Yes, if . . ."

Write a list of requests or asks you said "No, because" to in the past six months. Could your "No, because" become a "Yes, if"? Add the terms that would turn a "No" into a "Yes."

_____

_____

_____

_____

_____

_____

_____

_____

3
I Am . . .

I am *on a mission.*
Jenna Phillips Ballard

When my heart is racing as I am about to step on stage, or my tummy is doing back-flips as I am about appear on live television, or when I am in a difficult conversation (and I want to bring the loving Alicia and not the "I'm about to open a can of whoop-ass" Alicia), I say the following affirmation:

"I am a joyful, connected, and compassionate woman."

This is one of my many affirmations that I pull out of my tool kit when my amygdala is hijacked—when I feel sad, fearful, or angry, I have this simple sentence at the ready.

I know. I know. Affirmations can get a bad rap these days, lumped together with other self-help woohoo or new age mumbo jumbo. Or, you might believe they have a place in your personal life, but not at all in the business or corporate world.

But really, affirmations are a simple, powerful self-conversation starter that is appropriate for your personal, career, or love life.

If you just begin to utter the words "I am" with where you want to be or what you see for yourself, then magic can happen. For example, "I am healthy, wealthy, and wise," "I am strong and prepared iron man," "I am a collaborative leader," "I am a loving mom and wife." "I am . . . fill in the blank."

By creating affirmations, then you'll have them at the ready to support you in up-leveling life when self-limiting beliefs rear their ugly heads.

Act "as if"

"I am" is a statement that places *you* where you want to *be*. Your *mind* must arrive at a destination before your *life* does. These "I am" affirmations are a way to focus on where you want to be spiritually, emotionally, physically, and financially.

"I am" affirmations absolutely have a place in the business and corporate world. Take "I am committed . . ." for example. "I am committed to excellence in my current position and being promoted by the end of the year." "I am committed to preparing the exit strategy for my business and exiting in 18 months." "I am" affirmations become an integrity contract with yourself and those to whom you verbally commit.

Benefits

"I am" affirmations assist you in:

1. *Creating* your present and future self—on your terms
2. *Bridging* the gap between your critter brain and intelligent brain
3. *Focusing* on your vision for yourself and the world
4. *Grounding* as *source* energy—that you have the power to create what you want by dreaming, declaring, and delivering.
5. *Improving* your ability to be or become what you claim you are.

The power of the spoken word

I wrote about the *Abracadabra Principle* in my first book, and I have lived by the principle for over two decades. I have loosely defined *Abracadabra* as "what you say you create." No one is certain of the origination of Abracadabra. One theory is it's from the Aramaic 'avra kadavra,' meaning 'it will be created in my words.' And, of course, magicians use it as they reveal the finale of a magic trick.

What you say, you create. Using the power of the spoken word is how the spiritual realm, or source, is manifested in the physical world. I'm a strong believer in verbalizing written communication, such as journals, bucket lists, and your vision boards. Dream it, declare it, and deliver it, and so it shall be.

The Law of Action

There are 12 Universal Laws that are important to learn as you navigate the rugged seas of life. Here, we are going to focus on The Law of Action, in which certain actions must be employed in order for us to manifest things on earth. The Law of Action states that you must perform the actions necessary to achieve what you are setting out to do. Whether it's a small action of writing a to-do list, creating a vision board, or verbally declaring with an "I am" affirmation, like "I am committed," the universe will listen and conspire in your favor. Let's see this in action: Actor Jim Carrey wrote himself a check for $10 million dollars for "Acting Services Rendered" and gave himself three years, dating the check Thanksgiving 1995. Just before that date, he learned he was going make $10 million on his film project, *Dumb and Dumber.*

Lesson learned: If you can see it and believe it, you are on your way to achieving it.

I *Get* To . . . Write

Write your affirmations below. Then record a voice memo of yourself reading them. Listen to them as part of your meditation and journal writing routine.

I am _____.
I am _____.
I am _____.
I am _____.
I am _____.
I am _____.
I am _____.
I am _____.
I am _____.
I am _____.

Melissa Steach, I-O Psychologist, developed the following exercises to foster self-love in order to create great strides in your career.

• Write a love letter filled with career advice to your younger self, and feel free to use "I am" affirmations

- Get in groups of two or three and share (only what you want) about what you learned from writing the letter
- Volunteer to speak at the end about what you learned from listening to others' career advice

For a complete list and descriptions of *The 12 Universal Laws,* go to AliciaDunams.com/igetto to download the resource guide.

4
I'm committed to . . . vs. I'm trying . . .

Do. Or do not. There is no try.

Yoda

D o this: *Try* to count the amount of times you say "I'm trying" or "I'll try" in your daily language. Or:

Count the amount of times you say "I'm trying" or "I'll try" in your daily language.

Forget "I'm trying" or "I'll try," just do or do not, in the famous expression by Yoda.

Trying is failing with honor

When you use the words *trying* or *try,* you are subconsciously letting yourself off the hook for whatever you declare next.

Before you use "I'm trying" or "I'll try," ask yourself these questions:

- Are you setting yourself up for failure?
- Are you giving yourself a backdoor exit in case you don't accomplish your goals?
- Are you being lazy with your language, which, in turn, makes you lazy in your results?

"I'm trying" removes your responsibility. As the leader of your life, the ultimate come-from is "I am 100% responsible for it all."

Along with other examples of limiting language like "I can't" (Chapter 7), "I'm trying" convinces our subconscious mind that we shouldn't try, get started, or be able to accomplish something. When you turn it around and share "I am committed," it will train your subconscious mind to believe you can and will assist you in doing so.

Instead of using "I'm trying," use "I'm committed to"

As you step up your personal accountability game, instead of using "I'm trying," use "I'm committed." For example:

> "*I'll try* to have the paperwork signed by end of the week."

changes to . . .

"*I'm committed* to having the paperwork signed by Thursday at 6 pm."

And . . .

"I'm trying to lose 10 pounds by my wedding day."

changes to . . .

"I'm committed to losing 10 pounds by my wedding day, so I hired a personal trainer and hit the gym 5 times a week."

In both cases, the "trying" statement has no accountability. The "committed" statement has accountability and an action plan.

"I'm committed to . . ." statements are an opportunity to put skin in the game. During my workshops, I invite the participants to share a verbal commitment statement in the training room and publicly on social media. When you put skin in the game, not only do you hold yourself accountable, but your family, friends, and colleagues will hold you accountable as well.

And when you commit, then share. Share your commitments with your family and friends. Declare it out loud so the "universe has your back." Have your colleagues be your accountability buddies.

It's important to note that the words "I'm committed to" affect the outcome. When you complete your commitment, your self-esteem rises. Something I always say, "When we do acts of esteem, we improve our self-esteem."

A living example of commitment is Olympian Ruben Gonzalez, who is now a motivational and keynote speaker. He committed to train for the Olympics in the sport of luge. Everyone said it wasn't possible, that he was far too old to learn and train, and he'd be the oldest person out there. He couldn't find sponsors or even a country to compete for. But he did it because he was committed—he wouldn't accept any other possibility—and he first competed in 1988. He's competed four times in all, setting a record for Olympic luge competing.

Be impeccable with your word

When you state, "I'm committed to . . .," you are being impeccable with your word. That starts from making sure you're on time for meetings to making sure you are committed to what you say. When you commit and deliver on your commitments, you create trust.

My mentor, Dr. Betty Uribe, author of *#Values: The Secret To Top Level Performance In Business and Life* (Next Century Publishing, 2017), is a living example of integrity, commitment, and being impeccable with your word. Uribe walks her talk and does what she says she is going to do . . . from calling you when she says she will, to making introductions, to consummate follow-though. In her book, she shares how your commitment to your values creates trust, and we look to our leaders for just that.

> "When you think of someone you trust, most likely they live and lead according to their values. Two popular examples come to mind: Martin Luther King Jr., whose actions show his commitment to the good of the whole and to bettering the economic and social lives of a specific segment of the population, and Mother Teresa, a woman who led with integrity, focusing on the good of mankind and making a positive impact in others."

I *Get* To . . . Commit

During this exercise, write about your previous "I'm trying" or "I'll try" statements, and shift them to "I'm committed to" statements.
For example:

   "*I'll try* to . . .".

changes to . . .

   "*I'm committed* to . . . .".

5

**Specific date/
time vs. Someday**

*The Present way to Predict your Future is to
create it.*

Abraham Lincoln

I was in the most hilarious conversation with my
mom. It wasn't meant to be hilarious, but it ended
up being that way.

I was sharing a story about one of my friends
whose mother recently passed without a will in
place. All the mother's items were passed to my
friend's stepdad, even though my friend is an only
child. This caused a bit of a snafu for my friend
because her stepdad has kids from a previous mar-
riage. I mentioned this to my mom to encourage
her and my dad to complete their wills so nothing
like that would happen after she passed.

It's never fun talking about the subject of wills, but it's a necessary discussion. My mom said they had some of the initial paperwork done, but all they needed were a few signatures from the lawyer and the bank. I said, "Okay, by when would you have that complete?"

She paused and said, "Sometime this year."

I almost fell off my chair in laughter. Sometime this year? I said, "Mom, both you and dad are retired and, in between weekly games of pinochle, both of you have nothing going on but the rent." (Not exactly compassionate communication, but I was teasing and laughing with my mom.)

Sometime this year? I still laugh when thinking about this conversation.

In the game of business and changing the world, I encourage my clients and challenge myself to accomplish something significant on a daily basis. A few signatures would take no more than half a day. The fact that we put things off, continue to dwell on things left undone, or drag today's items into the next day or week's "to do" list is an unnecessary burden I would encourage you to stop doing to yourself. Use the time you have now to complete what you want to get done. From simple things like making your bed each morning to more significant things like following your business plan (or writing your will), it is well-documented that changing our daily habits change our weekly, monthly, and yearly outcomes.

I'm in the book coaching business, and my process is locked down to minutes and hours, not weekly and monthly deadlines. In Bestseller in a Weekend®, we complete exercises with timers. And when my students or clients complete these mini-sprints, they feel accomplished. And feeling accomplished feels *great.*

That's what we get to do with our life—be intentional with our communication and declare our deadlines whether it's written in our diary or announced to the world.

My invitation to you is to get specific with when you will be complete with items that are important to you.

If you want to create impact in your life, family, career, or in the world, then write down your dreams and goals with an explicit deadline. A "by when." A "do or die."

Nothing happens without a deadline.

"I'm going to write a book." By when?
"I'm going to start a business." By when?
"I'm going to apologize to my brother." By when?

"Someday" is not a line item on any calendar I know. Use intentional language to declare and deliver.

I *Get* To . . .Deliver

Declare items you are committed to creating in the next 30 days.

I am committed to _____
by _____. (Specific date and time)

I am committed to _____
by _____. (Specific date and time)

I am committed to _____
by _____. (Specific date and time)

I am committed to _____
by _____. (Specific date and time)

6
I choose to . . .

When we are no longer able to change a situation, we are challenged to change ourselves.
Victor Frankl

Every moment in our life is a choice moment. We have the freedom to choose, no matter the circumstance. Yes, I know there are circumstances in which people are in bondage, enslaved, in abusive relationships, or gravely ill . . . all situations where freedom and choices seem like a luxury. It might feel like they don't have choice moments, but they do. Here I defer to the words of Victor Frankl:

"Everything can be taken from a man but one thing: the last of the human freedoms—to choose

one's attitude in any given set of circumstances, to choose one's own way." Victor Frankl

. . . and

"The one thing you can't take away from me is the way I choose to respond to what you do to me. The last of one's freedoms is to choose one's attitude in any given circumstance." Victor Frankl

When you utter the words "I choose to," you command 100% responsibility for your life, and you make a commitment. Moment by moment, we get to choose what we want to create . . . so every moment is a decision point. You get to choose what type of person you want to be in that moment. You get to choose how you're going to communicate in the moment. You get to choose how you're going to act in the moment.

This is something powerful we can teach our children—that their life is not something that was set in stone, their destiny isn't final, and every moment they get to choose.

I *Get* To . . . Choose

List five things you choose to create in the next 30 days.

I choose to _____

I choose to _____

I choose to _____

I choose to _____

I choose to _____

7
**I can vs.
I can't**

*Whether you think you can or whether you
think you can't, you're right.*

Henry Ford

My Soul Cycle instructor believes it, and so does Barack Obama:

Yes You Can! Yes We Can!

Six little words that have inspired millions . . . from your early morning spin class instructor, your mentor at work, your porter as you transverse Mt. Kilimanjaro, and the former President of the United States.

Do yourself a favor: Use "I can" to start your sentences—it's the language of super heroes, triathletes, Nobel Award-winning scientists, and Oprah. Enough said.

"Can't" is a four-letter word, like a curse word. It damns you from a world of possibilities and opportunities. One of my most important lessons was not to use the statement "I can't." When you use that phrase, you immediately assume the role of victim.

When you feel the words "I can't" creeping into your vocabulary more and more often, respond with more positive language. Try saying "I choose not to" instead (Chapter 6). The word "choosing" implies action, purpose, and control. In using those words instead of "I can't," you quit playing the victim and assume responsibility.

Words are powerful. When you know the power of the spoken word, you become very careful in conversation. We must use words only to "heal, bless, or prosper." Just as it is powerful to speak positively, it is just as powerful to speak negatively. Negative words impress on our subconscious minds and ultimately create undesired feelings and results.

Through the spoken word, we create our own personal laws—laws of failure or success. I'll never understand why it's so easy for us to believe that the laws of failure apply, but so hard for us to trust that the laws of success are just as strong. It's about where we put our focus.

You believe it when you speak it aloud, such as when you say to yourself, "I can do this," rather than "I can't;" when you say to yourself, "Success is a reality," rather than "I'll never be able to succeed in this;" when you say to yourself, "I can achieve my dreams, and live the life I desire," rather than "I can't do that."

Words have the power to inspire, and then it only stands to reason that they also have the power to depress. Negative thoughts give birth to negative words, and negative words kill ideas, hopes, and inspirations.

It's all about how the subconscious mind serves to keep us from getting hurt—and it reinforces whatever we think. If we don't think we can lose weight, the subconscious mind isn't going to help us—it will remind us that we can't, so we won't disappoint ourselves.

"I can't do that."

"I can't afford that."

Let's use the last statement as an example.

"I can't afford that" carries many meanings. For example, it could mean "I do not have enough money or assets to my name to make it happen financially" or it could actually mean, "I can't emotionally handle it." In sales conversations, it usually pertains to a value proposition. Or, in the case that you are pursuing mansions in Malibu, a dream that cannot yet be realized. Energetically speaking, when you say you can't afford something, you tell the universe you can't afford it. I prefer shifting the conversation to, "I choose not to purchase that at this time." This creates a consciousness shift from thoughts of scarcity to a thought of choice.

What's next?

"I choose to create an action plan to create the money to purchase all I truly desire."

Or, more specific, is best:

"I choose to create a financial plan to save the money for a down payment to purchase an investment property in Los Angeles by December 31."

I *Get* To . . . Write

In your journal, list 10 "*I can't*" statements and shift them to *"I can"* statements. List what actions are required to make them happen.

For example, "I can't fix my credit" to "I can fix my credit." What is required is to contact a credit repair service, pay off my credit cards, and start budgeting my spending."

8
My request is . . .

Be a master asker.

Alicia Dunams

There's nothing like a formal request to call forth attention, discipline, and respect. I mean, when I hear, "Her Majesty requests your presence," I immediately want to straighten my back and adjust my regalia.

In a world where language is more casual than ever, formal requests are able to instantly cut through the BS of everyday babble to command respect and attention. This is true in the boardroom, in a coaching or leadership capacity, and in your day-in and day-out parenting.

"My request is . . ." is a sentence starter that sets the other party up to recognize that whatever you say next is of utmost significance.

- My request is you finish the report by Friday noon.
- My request is that you clean out the garage.
- My request is you attend this introductory event in order to be considered for this position.

I did a YouTube video about this very topic, and I had a comment that the words were commanding and perhaps confrontational. My response, "Yes, and the words must be used in a way to ensure the person being spoken to feels safe and regarded, and also compelled into action." There is a time and place for "My request is . . .".

"My request is . . . Will you honor my request?"

In my past, I have coupled "My request is . . ." with the following question, "Will you honor my request?" I used this sentence starter formula when I was a volunteer coach for a leadership program. The issue here is if someone doesn't honor your request, what do you do?

Asking the question, *Will you honor my request?* gives them the power to say "Yes" or "No." So, if that is the intention, to get a "Yes" or "No," then that question is fine. In my case of volunteering as a coach for a leadership program, the participants would 99% of the time come from Yes, because they were in the program to break-through the BS in their life. If they said "No", I would follow up with a clarifying question: "What were your reasons for enrolling into this leadership program?" This would get them clear on their intention and that I was there to be 100% in service.

Now, on the other hand, if you are setting a boundary that will not be crossed, do not follow the request with a "Yes" or "No" question, instead use this statement:

> "My request is we end this (conversation, interaction, etc.)."

Or, if they persist:

> "My request is we end this (conversation, interaction, etc.). I'm not available for this (conversation, interaction, etc.) now or ever."

If they continue to persist, remove yourself physically from the conversation.

That is a bold and unapologetic statement that sets a firm boundary. It shuts down the conversation.

You would not use this script if you and your spouse are going back and forth about where you are going on vacation, or whether you should refinance your home. That would look something like this:

"Hey babe, my request is we see my parents in Maine this summer as they are getting older and will be selling the summer home. Can we agree on that?"

This script is preferable because you're in dialogue with someone versus putting your foot down with the other script. Here, you make your request clear and also show you are amenable to a discussion.

I *Get* To . . . Request

Write a list of seven requests you have of others. Over the next week, call each person and request.

1. Name:_____Request: _____

2. Name:_____Request: _____

3. Name:_____Request: _____

4. Name:_____Request: _____

5. Name:_____Request: _____

6. Name:_____Request: _____

7. Name:_____Request: _____

9
Do you have a request?

A clever, imaginative, humorous request can open closed doors and closed minds.

Percy Ross

Sometimes people lack the ability to ask for what they want.

I've also had this issue once or twice or a 100 times. Once I was working with a coach, and we had a signed 12-month contract. About six weeks in, I felt our goals and tactics for my business were misaligned. For our next coaching call, I was thinking about ending the agreement, but I was unsure about my decision and couldn't quite make up my mind. On the call, I was having trouble mustering up the courage to ask for an end to our coaching agreement. I was humming and hawing, going around circles in the conversations, and creating incoherent babble.

He interrupted my indecisive thoughts and words by asking the following: "Do you have a request?"

That question hit me like a laser.

Questions hijack the brain. The moment you are asked a question, you can't think of anything else because your brain is programmed to answer questions immediately.

When communicating with someone who seems to be rambling and confused and the conversation has been misdirected, try asking the following question: "Do you have a request?"

"Do you have a request?" is a pattern interrupt. It supports people in getting to what they truly desire, yet haven't been able to articulate. People are looking for solutions and don't know how to dive into it.

When someone is verbally struggling to ask you something or you are unclear about their specific ask, this question creates an opportunity to have them slow down and receive the communication opening.

"Do you have a request?" not only supports the person who might be anxious or agitated, it also helps you as the receiver to harness the nervous energy and gain clarity.

"Do you have a request?" is also an interesting opportunity for people who may be intimidated by you or are afraid to give you feedback. By asking the question, you are giving them permission to share in a direct way that they may not have felt at liberty to do.

So, to finish my story, I said the following to my coach, "Yes, I do. My request is I would like to end our coaching contract and still remain friends."

He said, "Ok, that's all you had to say."

I *Get* To . . . Ask

Write your responses to the following prompts in your journal:

- Has there been a time in your life when you didn't ask for what you wanted?
- How would that circumstance or situation have shifted if the other person had said "Do you have a request?"
- If the universe asked, "Do you have a request?". . . how would you respond?

10

I acknowledge you . . .

The acknowledgement of a single possibility can change everything.

Aberjhani

Several years ago, my dad's twin sister, my Aunt Diane, died.

I didn't attend her funeral. I wrote it off as "I don't like funerals. Sure, funerals are a place to pay your respect to the deceased, to commune and commiserate with family and friends, and to celebrate life, but . . ."

My real reason is that I had many thoughts of shame and guilt because I didn't call and acknowledge my Aunt Diane when she was alive. I was too late. The reason I don't like funerals is that if

I didn't acknowledge that person when they were alive, what good is it to acknowledge them when they are dead?

So, my invitation to you is acknowledge people now, when they are alive and well, not when it is too late.

What you mean to me . . .

Never assume people know how you feel about them or how they impacted your life. Never leave anything unsaid. Show up for others in their time of need, and share words that will lift their spirits.

When you declare, "I acknowledge you," you dig down to find goodness in everyone. Using that script is a way to acknowledge people on how they showed up to you and the world. Again, you want to have your heart aligned with the words coming out of your mouth. My recommendation is to read the book, *The Art of Acknowledgement* by my mentor Margo Majdi, to learn about the power of acknowledgements. Margo has dedicated her life to acknowledging others from a place of deep gratitude and humility.

I *Get* To . . . Acknowledge

During this verbal exercise, acknowledge seven people in the next seven days—one per day. First write down the names of seven people you will acknowledge over the next seven days, and then write your thoughts on how you will acknowledge them:

1. Thoughts:

_____

_____

Name: _____

2. Thoughts:

_____

_____

Name: _____

3. Thoughts:

_____

_____

Name: _____

4. Thoughts:

_____

_____

Name: _____

5. Thoughts:

_____

_____

Name: _____

6. Thoughts:

_____

_____

Name: _____

7. Thoughts:

_____

_____

Name: _____

Whether you call them or meet them in person, you will acknowledge everyone you declared. Your life will change for the better, I promise!

11
I receive that

As we express our gratitude, we must never forget that the highest appreciation is not to utter words, but to live by them.

John F. Kennedy

Do you feel uncomfortable when someone acknowledges your or gives you a compliment?

Sometimes we get squirmy in our ability to accept and receive a compliment. But, "thank you" really works just fine. In Chapter 10, we learned about the power of acknowledgement. So, as with all energy, there is an ebb and flow, a give and take, and the acknowledge and receive.

When someone gives you a compliment or acknowledges you for a job well done, sometimes

we automatically give a compliment back to them—
which immediately diminishes the acknowledgements they are giving us. If someone is taking the
time to acknowledge you, you want to give him or
her the verbal cue that his or her compliment or
acknowledgment has been received by you.

Use: "I receive that." Or, simply: "Thank you."

That's all you have to say.

I *Get* To . . . Receive

Next time you get a compliment, just pause and
receive. Thank you.

12
It happened *for* me vs. It happened *to* me

The price of greatness is responsibility.
Winston Churchill

Are you being a victim to your circumstances, or are you being responsible for everything in your life? The way we answer the following question will determine the life we create:

Did it happen to me or did it happen for me?

What creates common ground between humans is that we are all going to have traumas, struggles, and obstacles. It's how we respond that counts.

There is a formula that I have used over a decade:

$$E + R = O$$

We cannot or will not ever be able to control events (E) or circumstances, but we are 100% able to control our response (R). This will create the final outcome (O).

Did it happen *to* me, or did it happen *for* me is a mindset script that you can ask yourself during times of challenge or struggle. Victim versus responsible? Did it happen *to* you, or did it happen *for* you? The way you see the world will determine your joy level. Guaranteed.

My mentor, Chris Lee, who travels the world supporting thousands of people in this life-changing reframe, shares a powerful story of what is possible when you shift the mindset from "it happened *to* me" to the mindset of "it happened *for* me."

A drunk driver killed the 18-year-old son of a mother when he came home from college to visit her for Christmas. The son's girlfriend lived on the same street. When he was walking back to his mom's house after visiting his girlfriend, the drunk driver plowed into him. He never made it home.

The mom was obviously filled with the most excruciating grief a parent can experience. Her grief was coupled with bitterness and anger toward the driver, and it was compounded by her anger toward the "system" that failed her too. She discovered the driver had multiple DUIs and offenses, so her bitterness intensified even more. She felt clearly wronged by this man who took her child and by the system that didn't take him off the streets.

Then she was diagnosed with cancer. Her anger and misery had manifested in her body. She realized that if she didn't change the way she saw this, if she continued being bitter and miserable in terms of coping with it, then she was pretty much dead too. You don't have to be in a coffin to be dead. But she was figuratively right there by her son.

She had to learn forgiveness.

So, she went to the jail and developed a relationship with the man. And eventually, she adopted his children. And her cancer is in remission.

So, the power of forgiveness . . .and recognizing that it happened *for* her, not *to* her . . . created her whole new life.

Did it happen to me or did it happen for me?

I use this reframe several times a day—for things great or small. For example, as I was writing this book, the initial writer/editor I hired got sick and didn't get started, and all of my other writer/editors were so busy with client work, I got to write this book myself—and I am so happy because I truly enjoyed the process. That would be a *small stuff* reframe.

Then there is *big stuff* reframe.

If you know my story, I have been a single mother with full custody of my daughter since she was a year old. Her biological father hasn't been a part of her life since then based on his choice and own abilities.

My daughter gets sad, even though she doesn't really know him. It's more of the feeling of void or expectations of what "could have been."

So, we have reframed this situation from did this happen to us or for us.

First, I share with her then reframe in the spiritual context that this is her cross to bear, just as Jesus bore a cross, and we all have a proverbial cross to bear. This is hers. Bearing a cross becomes your spiritual journey and your story to share and to teach. Bearing your cross opens you up to vulnerability, being relatable to others, and keeps you humble. I wouldn't have it any other way.

For a lighter reframe, we talk about being the 'Gilmore Girls,' and, because I have 100% custody, we were able to move to LA to pursue her modeling, acting, and singing.

When I was a younger single mom, I would have people encourage me to get married so she could have a step dad; otherwise, they said she would have "daddy issues." But the beauty of it all is that everyone has issues. I grew up with my mom and dad, and I have *both* daddy and mommy issues (said with a smile). I guess I wouldn't have it any other way.

Case in point, I heard of an experiment where they put 100 people in a training room, and the people were allowed to put all of their issues, traumas, and dramas on pieces of paper and place them in the center of the room. And, at the evening break, they could go to the center of the room and pick up anybody's issues. Guess what happens? People pick up their own stuff and happily transport it out of the room.

This is a really powerful reframe in terms of looking at your life—the past traumas, missteps, mistakes, obstacles, and "uh oh" moments. Rather than coming from a place of "It happened to me," that "My disease happened to me," or "This particular situation happened to me," try reframing, taking an awareness break, and asking yourself how it happened *for* you?

Every failure leads to success for those who don't give up.

I *Get* To . . . Reframe

In your journal, write a response to the following journal prompt.

What was a time in my life when I felt like a victim?

How did this experience happen *to* me?
What does it feel like to be a victim?
What thoughts, feelings and physical sensations come up?

Then ask yourself . . .

How did this experience change my life?
What opportunities came about because of this experience?
How has this experience brought me joy?
How did this experience happen *for* me?

13
I'm appointed vs. I'm disappointed

For the grateful, there is no room for disappointment;
Each moment offers life.

Unknown

Disappointment is a part of life. You don't get the role, your son drops out of college to join a rock band, and you are passed over for the promotion.

The definition of disappointment is the feeling of sadness or displeasure caused by the non-fulfillment of one's hopes or expectations.

Perhaps you are disappointed in other people. Maybe you are disappointed in yourself. Disappointment just exposes a gap in reality and expectations.

You didn't meet the mark, someone else didn't meet the mark, or a certain circumstance left you high and dry. When you are faced with a gap of this magnitude that causes you a disappointment, I invite you to turn it into an appointment.

What does that mean?

Well, simply delete the *DIS* from *DIS*appointment. The DIS that stands for disgruntled, disgusted, disease, discombobulated, etc. Just focus on the appointment.

The definition of appointment is an act of appointing; assigning a job or position to someone. Also known as a nomination or designation. Think of it this way: you are appointed King or Queen.

What does an appointment look like?

It's when you have an inkling, spiritual nudge, or intuitive hit to move forward and share your truth and story. That's what we're seeing with the #MeToo movement. Women coming forth, even after the statute of limitations is up, to share their truth. These women were hurt and disappointed about what these particular men did, and they are making it their responsibility to make wrongs right.

An example of this happened during one of my workshops. A participant had a medical issue where she was partially blind and could no longer read, and she was disappointed when she attended an event at her local community center, and they had a PowerPoint presentation with only words, so she couldn't read it. To add insult to injury, the event planners knew she would be in attendance, and didn't take the time or effort to adjust the presentation to be more inclusive.

"If they had just done a voiceover, I could have engaged in the presentation," she shared, disappointed. I said, "Okay, what would it look like if you made it an appointment? Instead of complaining about it, invite them to see that there are different perspectives, not everyone can read, and what could be changed? What would it look like if the presentation were available for people who could not read?" That's being appointed, rather than disappointed. That way, you're going to move from disappointed to appointed and give people the opportunity to improve. This is a leadership and learning opportunity.

If you have thoughts of disappointment, you can mentally see it as being appointed to take a stand for change moving forward. If you see it as someone doing something to you, you are a victim of the situation. For example, you are at a restaurant that you heard great things about, but the evening you are there you are disappointed with both the food and service. Instead of being disappointed and going home and slamming the restaurant on Yelp, which is absolutely available for you to do, what would it look like if you took a stand in that moment? What if you shared your experience with the manager and gave the restaurant the opportunity to course correct and make it right in the moment. That's why if my clients receive negative reviews on Amazon, I always coach them to respond in an open, receptive way saying they value the feedback and will address their concerns in a new edition of the book.

That is your call—to be a vessel to communicate this particular information to the person whom you might be "disappointed" with. You are appointed to make the world a better place.

Disappointment vs. appointment is a shift in power—shifting the power from the person who did "wrong" to the person who was "wronged," because now they have the power to use that experience in a positive way, to help others, increase awareness, etc.

I *Get* To . . . Appoint

Write about a time in your life when you were disappointed and how you turned it into an opportunity to take a stand for yourself and the other person or situation. Or, write about a time when you were disappointed and what steps you took to turn it into an appointment.

1) How can I use this experience to benefit or help others?

2) What lesson did I learn and how can it help me in the future?

3) What impact did I create for the other person or situation?

14

I call you forth, not out

What would you stand up for?

Oprah

Compassionate communication means to call people forth, not *out*. Give people the opportunity to come forth.

Call an individual forth in private rather than calling them out in public. What would it look like to call a co-worker forth? What would it look like to call a partner forth? What would it look like to call a child forth?

Here are some examples:

Spouse/Partner: Hey babe, I want to call you forth. I'm your partner to take a stand for you, me, and us. I notice that you are gossiping a lot with your friends. I know that's not you authentically, it's your small self, and I want to support you. Rather than being disappointed in your gossiping, I'm taking it on as my appointment to call you forth to stop.

Parent: My mom was reluctant to yell at her new stepdaughter about her messy room. So, instead of calling her out and being the mean stepmom, she wrote her stepdaughter a funny letter—a letter about a lost and forgotten floor. And she signed the letter, "Sincerely, Your Bedroom Floor." When my mom came home from work the next day, everything was picked up and put away, and they all had a good laugh.

I have seen a trend of business influencers who are publicly outing, perhaps shaming, other business influencers in public forums, such as Facebook, blogs, emails, and other social media channels.

We've seen this trend for years with consumers outing Fortune 500 companies, like the attention directed at Dove for an insensitive advertising campaign. A colleague recently called out a software company on Facebook LIVE for having poor customer service. The Internet has normalized this behavior.

But what if the outing is not of an organization or company, but of another human being?

For example:

> I heard of a four-year riff between a NY Times bestselling author, who has a solid online business, and another online business partner. The issue was plagiarism of a landing page.
>
> I heard about a consultant calling out her business coach, who is a popular author and persona, by saying she is not practicing what she preaches and has an "ineffective business model."

I can see how, in some cases, this "calling out" may be considered a public service announcement to warn others of perceived or verified acts of wrongdoing, such as:

- Plagiarism
- Lack of integrity
- Shoddy work
- Poor customer service
- Fraud/scam
- Stealing ideas/clients/employees
- Not being a nice person

Is there a more courageous way to "call people out?" Yes! It's to "call people forth!"
Here's the distinction:

> When we "call people out": It can be experienced as an attack, public shaming, and bullying; it can create online "rubber necking," schadenfreude, and drama; it can be experienced as someone

making someone look bad in order to make themselves look good; it becomes a "me/us" against "you/them" game.

When we "call people forth": It can be experienced as taking a stand . . . for yourself and the other person; it can create an environment of collaboration, growth, vulnerability, and connection; it gives people an opportunity to take responsibility, apologize, and make things right; it can create a win/win society.

From my perspective, calling people forth is a leadership distinction that brings people together, while calling people out creates further divisions.

To clear or not to clear

Clearing is a practice of radical honesty. You share with a person what is coming up for you, and you take 100% responsibility for those thoughts, feelings, and physical sensations. There is no blame or shame in this exercise. Just 100% responsibility on your part, which will create openings for the other party. For example, perhaps you had a riff with your sibling. There is tension, and you decide the only way out is through. You call them up and say, "I know there is tension between us since last Easter, and I want to clear it with you. I take responsibility for not being forthright in the beginning and letting this go on for so long."

I *Get* To . . . Call People Forth

In your journal, write about the following prompts:

- Have you called someone out publicly or privately? How can you call them forth?
- Is there someone in your life you get to clear with? Who is it? How can you take 100% full responsibility?
- Call this person and open to opportunity to clear.

15
Let's shift the conversation

Each person does see the world in a different way. There is not a single, unifying, objective truth. We're all limited by our perspective.
Siri Hustvedt

I have become increasingly aware how useful guided interruption is as a tool.

One of the best interrupters is popular podcaster James Altrucher, who interrupts with a purpose to diverge the stream of thought when people are diving deep into a topic on his podcast, 'The James Altucher Show."

In technology, disruption is celebrated. Netflix disrupted Blockbuster. Then Netflix went on to disrupt itself. (Remember when we used to return Netflix CDs in red self-addressed envelopes?)

In technology, we are in the era of reiteration and course correction. Should our personal conversations be any different?

Disruption is to technology as interruption is to a conversation.

Someone may interrupt a conversation because they are so excited to interject something, and they can't wait for you to pause or breathe. Others may interrupt because they have a correction to add or important detail to interject.

Which begs the question: How can redirection put misdirected or undirected conversations back on track?

Interruption and redirection are an art.

For example, political conversations are a great time to use the sentence starter, "Let's shift the conversation . . ."

Everyone is around the water cooler the next day after a presidential debate or another national event that invites questions, comments, and considerations. The conversation gets political and tension fills the air. You, because you are well-equipped after reading "I *Get* To," chime in and say:

> "Look, we are a modern office with diverse opinions and perspectives. I invite that we hold space for everyone's opinion which has been shared, and that *we* shift the conversation."

If the conversation is going sideways or to an area that you don't want to discuss, it's an opportunity to create a boundary. As seen in the previous example, it's not only *you* that's setting the boundary, you are suggesting that the collective is setting the boundary by using "we" language "Let's shift the conversation" or "we shift the conversation."

You want to use "we" language so you can create engagement and a collective decision moving forward.

Some people may not want to shift the conversation and want to continue in the banter, even though divisive. This is when you can hold firm with your boundary and say:

> "My invitation was for us to collectively shift the conversation. Since it feels like it's still moving forward with no change, I choose to respectfully opt out."

I *Get* To . . . . Shift the conversation

Write in your journal the following:

What are your signals or red flags that a conversation must be shifted for the greater good of the team or group?

16
Cancel,
cancel . . .

I am a blank slate - therefore I can create
anything I want.

Tobey Maguire

Ever put your foot in your mouth, and you would do anything to erase what you said? Maybe you said something to offend another person, maybe a conversation started going sideways, or maybe you uttered words that cut yourself down, such as "I can't do that" or "I can't afford that."

Let's use the that last statement as an example.

"I can't afford that" carries many meanings, as mentioned in Chapter 7. For example, "I do not have enough money or assets to my name to make it happen financially." Energetically speaking, when you say you can't afford something you tell the universe it's out of your reach. I prefer shifting the conversation to, "I choose not to purchase that at this time." So, in case you say, "I can't afford that," Immediately say, "Cancel, cancel," and then say, "I choose not to purchase that at this time."

My mentor Margo Majdi taught me that the words "Cancel, cancel" are a magic eraser. "Cancel, cancel" creates a clean slate and a new moment. If you've said something that you regret saying or you want a complete rewind, use "Cancel, cancel." This verbally tells the universe, "Erase what I just said. Can I start over?" If you feel silly muttering "Cancel, cancel," you can actually say, "Can I start over?" if the conversation is going in the wrong direction.

For example, there was a week when my daughter and I got in a verbal spar every day about her room not being clean or some other typical teenager/parent conversation. We promised each other we would not fight again, but again we started down the road of anger, idle threats, and sayings like, "when you graduate from high school, you're on your own. I'm moving to Costa Rica!"

So I said to her, "Cancel, cancel, let's rewind. Can I have a do over?"

It disarmed the situation and gave us a chance to laugh at ourselves and start from scratch.

In a business situation, use this statement to admit things may be going in the wrong direction—we got off on the wrong foot, etc. For example, you are giving feedback to a colleague and you didn't acknowledge him or her first, as I suggest in Chapter 19. So, you jumped right into feedback:

"Your report was not well received by the leadership committee."

You see that your colleague is not taking it well. Pause. How can you make this a redo?

"Cancel that. May I start over? First, I want to acknowledge you on the advertising campaign last week. We are getting great feedback, and I know the quality work you do. You are an asset to our team. So, there is some opportunity for growth on the leadership committee report. We got feedback that it missed the mark, so my request is that you take another shot so it's more in alignment with your previous work."

These examples show what is possible when you stop going down a wrong road, flip a U-turn, and clean up any miscommunication at the time and start from a blank slate.

Just as in the previous example, when someone agrees to cancel and start over, you've avoided a potentially bad outcome. Additionally, you have rewound and redirected the conversation so there are no misunderstandings or misconceptions. You have removed the potential for negative emotions and hurt feelings.

What if they do not agree to a "Cancel, cancel" or a redo? (Oh gosh, I dislike "What if" statements . . . see Chapter 18). What if they say no and the conversation starts to get out of hand and emotionally charged?

My suggestion is the following:

PAUSE.

Let the flight or fight response that is flooding both of your brains cease and take a breather. Perhaps you ask for a moment.

And, when the space allows, state the following:

"I am personally starting over so we can create a shift in this conversation. First, I want to acknowledge you for . . . (You want to be open and genuine in this acknowledgement.). It's important we proceed with a win/win."

I *Get* To . . . Cancel

Was there a time in your life where you wish you said "Cancel, cancel". . . where you wanted to rewind and redo a moment to improve a relationship with a family member, friend, or colleague? Write it below:

_____

_____

_____

Want to rewind and redo?

Cleaning up the past is important to move forward with no regrets. Write a letter or pick up the phone. Acknowledge them, take responsibility, and create a collective stand or contract moving together.

Collective "We" Contract:

For Example:

We, _____ and _____, choose to be honest and listen to each other.

We, _____ and _____, choose to be _____ and _____.

17
Yes, AND . . .

Always say 'yes' to the present moment . . .
Surrender to what is. Say 'yes' to life - and see
how life starts suddenly to start working for
you rather than against you.

Eckhart Tolle

K ill the word "But."
Why?

Because the word "but" cancels out or contradicts everything that precedes it. And if you say "but" to someone who comes to you with a fresh idea, you instantly negate the validity of the idea and shut him or her down.

"Most people just want to be validated and heard," says Maxine Shapiro, facilitator, coach and founder of Collaborcate!™. Maxine takes applied improvisation, which originates from theater improv, and brings it to the business, team, and personal development world.

"In a lot of organizations, you've got executives who stand there with their arms folded like Mr. Clean, who demand, 'Come to me with your ideas,'" Shapiro states. "People eagerly come to them with their ideas, and they get the 'whoosh'— the arm waves, and their idea is quickly dismissed, 'That's not going to work! Give me another idea.' Well, you know what, you just shut me down. I'm not going to come to you with another idea."

Here's a sneak peak of "Yes, and . . .," the golden rule of improv:

During a "Yes, and . . ." exercise, you agree with what your partner says and build their thoughts, ideas, and concepts by using the conversation starter "Yes, and . . . ." Turn by turn, both partners continue to build upon what each person adds to the brainstorming/ideation conversation.

"It's best to start this exercise with something that is not work-related. You already have limiting beliefs and triggers regarding the business issue. So, start with pairs. A & B. B starts by saying, 'Let's take a trip!' A: Yes, and let's fly to Paris. B: Yes, and we can take a French Pastry cooking class. A: Yes, and we can become world renown chefs because of a secret ingredient.' Just like any new muscle, you have to exaggerate the "Yes, and . . ." exercise. I like to add, money is not an object and, sometimes, the law of physics do not apply. Play with it."

In his interview in *Fast Company* magazine, Kelly Leonard, author of *Yes, And: How Improvisation Reverses "No, But" Thinking and Improves Creativity and Collaboration--Lessons from The Second City* (Harper Business, 2015) states, "What you learn about improvisation when you apply 'Yes, and' is that there's a bounty of ideas, way more than will ever get used. Everyone in the ensemble produces hundreds of ideas, so even though most of (the ideas) will die and never be seen again, people don't hold on out of fear that they'll have nothing to offer at the end." (Hugh Hart, "Yes, And . . . 5 More Lessons In Improving Collaboration and Creativity From Second City," www.fastcompany.com, February 26, 2015, https://www.fastcompany.com/3042080/yes-and-5-more-lessons-in-improv-ing-collaboration-and-creativity-from-second-city)

Shapiro reminds us that, if leaders want to keep an organization moving forward, they must be open to new and different options. "Yes, and . . ." can take you there, all while capturing a more engaged employee. Shapiro emphasizes, "This process is critical in recruiting and keeping the best of the millennial talent. Organizations really don't have a choice anymore."

On a side note, since an early age, my daughter Izzy has been an actor and a master at improv. She has these skills mastered, whereas I, on the other hand, am just getting started. She pointed out in one of my video interviews that I continued to say the word "but," and by doing so didn't set my interviewee up to win. (Love getting business feedback from a teen.) It's because of this that I've become fascinated by the improv tool, "Yes, and . . ."

I *Get* To . . . Say "Yes, and"

For the next seven days, play the game, "Yes, and . . ." in every interaction with a colleague or friend that comes to you with an idea. In your journal, write what opens up for you and others in the process.

18
Why not . . . vs. What if . . .

*Some men see things as they are and ask why.
I dream of things that never were and ask why
not.*

Robert Kennedy

In a video clip of one of his seminars, famed author and motivational speaker, Jim Rohn declared, *'What if' is the language of the poor!*

My biggest story around "What if . . ." came when I decided to backpack around the world in 1998. I was 22 years old, and a good percentage of my friends and family frantically thought I was going to be raped, kidnapped, or murdered . . . or all three. (Mind you, this was before cell phones and when the Internet was just starting to be a thing.)

I heard:

> What if you get lost?
> What if you lose your passport?
> What if you get sick?

I left anyway and sailed through the South Pacific, trekked through Nepal and India, road camels in Morocco, and got my passport confiscated at the American Embassy in London. Just shy of a year later, I returned to California completely unscathed and 20 pounds heavier, with a farmer's tan, very calloused feet, and a trunk load of memories.

And I'll say this: I did get lost. I did lose my passport (on a technicality). I did get sick (avoid yak cheese pizza in Nepal). I also missed a plane, almost severed a finger, got conjunctivitis, and jumped out of a plane. And I survived. Actually, I *thrived*.

Along with having my daughter, that solo around-the-world trip was one of the top experiences in my entire life.

Fast forward, two decades later, I still hear "What ifs . . ." about everything from going on vacation to starting a business.

"What if . . ." crushes dreams like no other statement if it's stated in the negative. It has been used as the statement of overly concerned parents, haters, other dream crushers, and even from the dark corners of your own thoughts. On the other hand,

"What if . . ." could serve as an opening to the possibilities it has the potential to possess.

If "What if . . ." were assigned a Thinking Trap, it would be the following:

Catastrophizing (also known as fortune-telling): You predict the future negatively without considering other, more likely outcomes.

"What if you fail?" One way you could respond is, "What if I succeed?" That opens up the conversation to possibility and potential, rather than anxiety and apprehension.

Why not?

Karen Reitvich, a leading expert in the fields of resilience, depression prevention, and Positive Psychology, is the Director of Training Programs for the Penn Positive Psychology Center. She has three strategies to challenge negative Thinking Traps when they're actually happening in my (or your) mind.

1. Evidence:

That's not true because . . . (Find evidence to the contrary)

2. Reframe:

A more helpful way to see this is . . . (This would be the "Why not")

3. Plan:

If "X" happens, I will "Y"

Let's put this into action to demonstrate how to be better equipped to respond to someone who questions you about a decision like traveling around the world, for example.

1. Evidence:

I have talked to two friends who have traveled around the world solo, and they had the most fantastic time. One even met her husband. It was a life-changing experience.

2. Reframe:

A more helpful way to see this is as a once-in-a-lifetime trip and a way of following my dream. I'm thankful that you care about me, and I am committed to being smart and safe with all my decisions.

3. Plan:

- If I get lost, I will go to the closest police station, grocery store, or gas station and ask for assistance.
- If I lose my passport, I will contact the American Embassy or go to its website to find next steps.
- If I find myself in trouble, I will dig deep to find the safest way out.

And to tell you the truth, many of these things and more did happen to me. Once when I was traveling through the island of Fiji late at night, I hired a taxi from the bus station to go to a youth hostel. The ride was fine at the beginning, but then the driver headed the car into a field of sugarcane. He pulled over, and I asked what he was doing, and he said, "I have some beer in the back." He then reached into the back seat to get a grocery bag of beer. Calmly, I looked him in the eyes and said, "I know what you are thinking, and it's wrong, and you are not going to do it."

He looked at me, put the bag in the back seat, and then drove away from the sugarcane field and to the youth hostel as planned.

I pulled that conversation starter, or stopper in this case, from the archives of my mind. Back when I was an intern at HBO Pictures in LA during college, I had a very astute and powerful boss. She shared the story of when a man broke into her house and approached her when she was cooking in the kitchen. She felt a presence, turned around in shock, and said to him what I later said to the driver: "I know what you are thinking, and it's wrong, and you are not going to do it."

Of course, these are two unique situations. For your personal safety, I invite you to dig deep for what you feel is the best thing to do in whatever situation you may find yourself.

An alternative perspective

I just shared descriptions and examples of "What if . . ." used in the negative. However, there is a potential positive use of "What if . . .," as suggested by Amy Hill, I-O Psychologist with a certification Equine Assisted Learning (EAL). "For example, in the workplace, when you use 'What if . . .' as a preface to an idea or suggestion for your colleagues, you preserve others' egos and reduce emotion because you're simply in a state of curiosity, not one of forcing your position," suggests Hill. "This enables colleagues to brainstorm more easily with you."

Here's another positive example of "What if . . ." in the workplace. Hill expands: "Often there is a primary driver for companies to make a physical workplace change, whether it's lease expirations, attracting better talent, or cost reduction. Questions such as, 'What if we could deliver a workplace experience that not only attracts talent, but also amplifies our corporate culture? What would that look like?' expand the possibilities beyond the initial goal and creates a spirit of co-creation."

I *Get* To . . . Reframe

Now, turn your "What if" into a "Why not." List three "What ifs" and write examples of your evidence, reframe, and plan to turn it from negative fortune telling to a positive outcome.

What if:
- Evidence
- Reframe
- Plan

What if:
- Evidence
- Reframe
- Plan

What if:
- Evidence
- Reframe
- Plan

For a complete list and descriptions of *Thinking Traps,* go to AliciaDunams.com/igetto to download the resource guide.

19
Are you open to feedback?

There is no failure. Only feedback.
Robert Allen

"Feedback gets a bad rap these days," says Melissa Steach, I-O Psychologist. "In corporate cultures, feedback has been seen as a way for people to criticize others, rather than a way to provide valid constructive feedback to support others in their interactive growth. When an employee hears the word 'Feedback,' they may shutter." Steach continues, "Due to this trigger, the word has even been replaced by 'FeedForward' as people request constructive versus deconstructive criticism to propel their personal and business development forward."

Another way to counter this fear of feedback is to ask permission to give it, with the simple conversation starter, "Are you open to feedback?"

My mentor, Victor Cheng (www.VictorCheng.com), is a master at corporate communications, and, in particular, giving productive and neutral feedback.

Cheng states, "How feedback is received by the other party is highly dependent on the relationship, including any kind of implied or explicit agreements between the two people. From my standpoint, it's not just the phrase or intonation of the feedback, but what was the expectation set early on in the relationship."

To set up a relationship to win and to ensure the other person knows that receiving feedback will be a part of the relationship (or, in this case, the job description), Cheng sets up the following scenario:

> "We are a high-performance organization, and we are committed to getting better and doing better. My job is to help you get better, and your job is to make me better, and our job do better for our clients. Our job is to be better in the marketplace, and part of that goal is providing feedback."

Pretty straightforward.

In addition to setting the expectation that feedback is part of the job experience, Cheng suggests having the standard of performance documented and explained in writing and provided in advance of the working relationship.

"Feedback is not about judgment," Cheng states. "You are pointing out that the performance of the person does not match the standard of performance that was articulated in writing at the beginning of the working relationship."

Wise feedback

In his book, *The Culture Code: The Secrets of Highly Successful Groups,* Daniel Coyle cites research from the "Journal of Experimental Psychology" (April 2014) about breaking the cycle of mistrust and providing feedback across the racial divide. In that research, teachers prefaced their feedback to students with the following statement:

"I'm giving you these comments because I have very high expectations and I know that you can reach them."

This statement created a space of belief, trust, belonging, and high standards. That's what you call "wise feedback."

Sometimes a request for feedback is outside the parameters of work performance standards, such as when a co-worker wants feedback on some personal issues or is looking for feedback on a draft document or email they are about to send. After you listen to them or review their work, you can use the following communication starter, "Are you open to a suggestion?" This way you give your thoughts as a suggestion, not a determination. You are not attached to whether they use the suggestion or not, because you make it clear that the final decision is up to them.

Are you open to feedback?

Cheng is well-versed in feedback in corporate environments. He knows what works in corporate settings does not necessarily work in intimate relationships or small group dynamics because more personal experiences and perspectives are at play.

For example, if your wife and you have an agreement that says if either of you are going to be 30 or more minutes late, you will call in advance. If your wife shows up four hours late with no call, and you say, "You are late. That does not match the standard of performance" . . . well, that would not go over well.

In this case, you would want to bring forth vulnerability and awareness, and share that you feel unworthy, unloved, or whatever is true for you when your spouse/partner shows up late without letting you know.

One of the ways I provide feedback is asking in a gentle way, "Are you open to feedback?"

When I ask my teenage daughter this, she usually rolls her eyes but immediately says, "Yes." Her immediate "Yes" is because she knows the conversation is taking a more intimate and significant turn—something worthy of turning away from her smart phone to listen.

When I ask this question to my hubby ("hubby" is my pet-name for my life partner . . . and his for me is "wifey"). I see him shutter a bit, but then he is dying to hear what I have to say. It provides a bit of mystery, depending on my intonation.

To take the edge off the question, I will be playful with both my daughter and hubby beforehand. Like to my hubby, "My love, are you open to some feedback?" This creates some mystique because of the playful nature and intonation.

The results are always the same: Both my hubby and Izzy end up dying to hear my feedback.

I also acknowledge people before I provide feedback. Acknowledgement first helps the person on the receiving end of the feedback to be open to receive and not feel like they're being personally attacked. Here are some examples:

"I acknowledge you for _____ and . . ." (Use AND vs. BUT as in Chapter 17)

   ". . . my experience is you are shut down when we discuss _____ (topics)

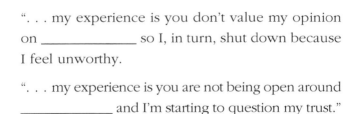

". . . my experience is you don't value my opinion on _____ so I, in turn, shut down because I feel unworthy.

". . . my experience is you are not being open around _____ and I'm starting to question my trust."

". . . my experience is you are not respecting my boundaries, and I want to ensure we hold these safe so we can grow closer."

In these examples, your experience is your perspective. If you remember one thing, remember this: **All feedback will be given through the filter of perspective, beliefs, and biases**.

Even if you are on the receiving end of feedback, always know feedback is tainted through that person's perspective.

In addition to providing acknowledgement as well as your perspective, it's best to give feedback by using the "sandwich method." This way, you state what worked, then what didn't work, and then summarize what worked again or add an acknowledgement or another example of what worked. It's always a good thing to end on any feedback on a positive note.

If they say no

When you ask someone if they are open to feedback and they say "no," that is feedback *to you* that your intonation or delivery didn't create a space of opening or safety. In other words, that person is not feeling safe because you did not make him or her feel safe. They may have a feeling of judgment, insecurity, or fear.

So, if they say "no," take time to notice your way of being, and know you are complete. Don't insist on providing feedback anyway. Instead, use this as a time to journal what your truth in that moment is and what you can learn from it.

I *Get* To . . . Acknowledge and provide feedback

Acknowledge and provide constructive feedback to one person today.

Name: _____

"I acknowledge you for _____ and . . ."

". . . my experience is _____ (topics)

20
What worked . . .
and what didn't
work . . .

The most serious mistakes are not being made
as a result of wrong answers. The truly dan-
gerous thing is asking the wrong question.

Peter Drucker

At the end of every year, I go on a retreat
somewhere and make an assessment of the
year. Instead of saying what was good about the
year or what was bad about the year I ask, "What
worked" and "What didn't work?"

This is a great tool for self-evaluation, like after
you speak in front of a group, ask yourself, "What
worked" and "What didn't work?"

I do this for my personal relationships as well,
and for the yearly review I do it with my daughter

and my hubby. That way you focus on and are grateful for the things that did work, and then you can think about what didn't work and find a solution for that.

"What worked" and "What didn't work" are also great for:

- Employee evaluations
- Client evaluations (If you are a speech coach, perhaps you want to give feedback to your client who just went up on stage.)
- Feedback for your children
- Self-evaluations
- An intimate conversation with your spouse/partner about your relationship the prior 12 months.

Good and bad

I'm not a fan of the words "Good" or "Bad" as the words good and bad imply moral judgment. Any words that judge can create division. Also, who decides what is "Good" or "Bad"?

Case in point, murder is definitely "bad," but we also have evidence that murder is legal and "good" for humankind in States with the death penalty. So, how is it bad on one account and not another? This is where perspective comes in.

What worked and what didn't work is a better fit for feedback than good or bad. Remember, all feedback will be given through the filter of perspective, beliefs, and biases.

I *Get* To . . . Understand

In your journal, at the end of the day, assess what worked and didn't work.

Relationships:
   What worked?
   What didn't work?

Career:
   What worked?
   What didn't work?

Lifestyle:
   What worked?
   What didn't work?

Relationships:
   What worked?
   What didn't work?

21
What landed
for me . . .

An investment in knowledge pays the best
interest.

Benjamin Franklin

Some positive feedback I have received in my career is that I am a "great synthesizer." Basically, they meant that I can take a variety of facts, information, and experiences from different sources and distill it into manageable chunks. (I hope I am doing an ok job at that in this book.)

One way to be a great synthesizer is to reiterate what you have learned, whether it's from a text, workshop, seminar, or feedback, by stating the following: "What landed for me is . . ." and then list all of the key points and takeaways.

One thing I do in my workshops is ask participants, "What landed for you?" And around the room,
people will answer with what landed for them. This
is a great way for participants in the room to learn
from other perspectives about what landed, and
it's also a great way to be reminded of key points.
By doing so, people can synthesize what they just
heard in addition to letting you know what landed
for them. If you run workshops or lead business
meetings, I suggest using this as an exercise to hear
what is landing for people. This provides feedback
for you as a business professional and as a colleague.

Another way to think about using "What landed
for me . . ." is "What hit home for me . . ." or
"What resonated for me. . . ." This is an effective
way to take notes at seminars, workshops, or meetings. It's also effective to share notes among fellow
colleagues, so each can experience the experience
through everyone's lens.

I *Get* To . . . Share What Landed For Me

After you attend another workshop, corporate
training, or conference call, share with the group
the key points and takeaways that landed for you
by using the conversation starter, "What landed
for me. . . ."

22
. . . (The pause)

Silence is a true friend who never betrays.
Confucius

Early on in my business, when I was first learning about front of the room sales (aka "selling from the stage" techniques), I really resisted the formulaic structure. It required that you introduce yourself, say what you were going to share over the next 30 to 45 minutes, provide value, share your story, show how said strategy helped you, demonstrate how said strategy would help the members of the audience, and then finally make an offer that people could invest in with you. Part of the strategy was to pause at key moments in your sales presentation to give the audience a moment to process what you said, let a key "a-ha" sink in, or allow space for emotions and reactions to build.

I hated those moments. I would feel uncomfortable and my heart would race . . . I thought surely it was beating loud enough for others to hear in this awkward period of time we all shared. The silence and suspense of the pause would kill me. I would usually do something to fill the uncomfortable space like crack a joke or ask the audience if they had any questions. I couldn't let the pause just live there all alone, I needed to fill the space.

This problem also spilled over into my phone sales technique, which also includes a bit of finesse and particular way of asking questions, gathering information, gaining insight, and pausing to listen for key phrases in the response.

A few years into my business, I hired business sales strategist and TV pitch coach, Sanyika Calloway, to support me with this process.

She always said in TV you must respect the "pregnant pause" (meaning you don't just want to pause, you want your pause to be nine months pregnant . . . well, not literally, but that's what it felt like to me!). What she was really trying to express is there is value and purpose and even necessity in the pause. It communicates far more than words ever could.

The power of the pause

Communication isn't just words. Effective communication includes non-verbal communication.

The power of the pause allows you to process, gain perspective, and gather your thoughts instead of blurting out the first thing that comes to mind.

A non-verbal pause gives your words power, just like the pauses in music . . . the spaces in between the notes that create the beautiful sounds. The pauses in speaking create opportunities for more beautiful language.

When you are triggered in any way or engaged in a difficult and emotionally charged conversation, you want to pause (maybe by taking one deep breath in and letting it out), and then speak from a place of clear, concise communication. You could also give a physical cue, such as putting one hand over the other, momentarily closing your eyes, or clearing your throat.

Remember, your brain is programmed to answer questions immediately. It's an Automatic Response as we discussed in the book's introduction.

Pausing after someone asks you a question is a conscious choice and requires you to override what you would instinctually and automatically do. It does not make you look less intelligent, dim-witted, or "off your game." On the contrary, pausing gives you perspective and allows you to respond in a way that needs no explanation or apology. If you have ever "spoken out of turn" or "shot off at the mouth," you know what I'm talking about and hopefully see the power of the pause as a profound gift.

Three benefits of pausing in sales scenarios

In his prolific works, Brian Tracy says that pausing before you speak has three specific benefits. Let's review each one.

Listening builds trust

Pausing gives you the space to avoid interrupting the other person so they feel heard. It also provides you with time to gather more information about your potential client. When you listen, people trust you.

Careful consideration shows you care

The second benefit of pausing is that your silence tells the prospect you are being mindful of what they are saying. That shows you care and is a significant compliment that raises self-esteem.

Understanding creates greater efficiency

The third benefit of pausing before replying is that you'll have time to reflect on the words being said. That gives you time to look for the true meaning behind the words and provide more personalized solutions and service.

I *Get* To . . . Pause

Silence isn't empty . . . it's full of answers. So, I invite you to take a three-second pause after every interaction this week. Then notice how different your interactions were. You might even be inspired to ask a friend to join you in this "pause challenge" and provide feedback so you can find out how they experience you and this intentional change in communication.

23
You may
think that . . .

To be persuasive we must be believable; to be
believable we must be credible; to be credible
we must be truthful.

Edward R. Murrow

In 2012, I enrolled in the yearlong business mastermind, Ascended Masters, which was facilitated by Silicon Valley executive coaches Bryan Franklin and Jennifer Russell. Every two months or so, 30+ entrepreneurs would gather for experiential mastermind retreats in San Francisco, Silicon Valley, New York City, and forested areas in between. During our New York City retreat, author Michael Ellsberg, the event's guest lecturer, shared his strategy for writing a compelling book proposal.

On the heels of the success of his book, *The Edu-cation of Millionaires* (Portfolio, 2012), Ellsberg was in the midst of writing his second proposal, so he generously shared the persuasive writing technique he had learned from Franklin that compelled publishers to purchase *The Education of Millionaires* and his title-in-progress.

This persuasive writing technique is called: Clear Story Format.

Clear Story Format is a communication starter technique that supports the user to bust myths, preconceptions, and biases. Bryan Franklin invented Clear Story Format for the purposes of training executives and entrepreneurs to be more influential.

To explain Clear Story Format, first I'll reveal the structure as follows:

1. **You may think that** ...
2. **but really** ...
3. **If you just** ...
4. **Then** ...

I will show it in action with an excerpt from Ellsberg's book proposal for *The Last Safe Investment*, which was co-authored by Bryan Franklin and published by Penguin/Random House in 2016.

You've been fed a lie. The lie is that if you scrimp and save for decades, refusing to spend on yourself, and then invest the money you've saved into 401(k)s, IRAs, mutual funds, and index funds, and borrow to buy a home, these investments will grow steadily over decades—allowing you 20 to 30 years of secure, peaceful inactivity at the end of your life.

This may have been true at some point in the last century. But it is not true any longer.

If you want to get ahead and enjoy a life of prosperity, then you must invest in the most powerful—yet rarely discussed—source of wealth you'll ever know: your own earning power.

Here's the proposal sample with Clear Story Format detailed:

You may think that . . .:
You've been fed a lie. The lie is that if you scrimp and save for decades, refusing to spend on yourself, and then invest the money you've saved into 401(k)s, IRAs, mutual funds, and index funds, and borrow to buy a home, these investments will grow steadily over decades—allowing you 20 to 30 years of secure, peaceful inactivity at the end of your life. This may have been true at some point in the last century.

but really . . . (Note: Remember, we learned in Chapter 17 that the word "But" cancels out all that preceded it.)

But it is not true any longer.

If you just . . .
If you want to get ahead and enjoy a life of prosperity,

Then . . .
then you must invest in the most powerful—yet rarely discussed—source of wealth you'll ever know: your own earning power.

As we see in the example, the Clear Story Format works for explaining concepts and ideas to others who might reject new ideas, be resistant to change, or have biases.

To that end, Clear Story Format is great for writing book proposals and other persuasive writing styles, as shown above. Additionally, Clear Story Format is a perfect verbal medium enrollment tool, such as pitching in front of the room. I recently used the format when I was spontaneously asked to pitch my business in front of a room of female scientists. Overall, it's an effective skill for business writing or presenting a clear call to action.

Clear Story Format for interpersonal relationships

Bryan shares the Clear Story Format in an intimate setting:

You might think that sharing more of yourself is what creates the feeling of intimacy (not physical intimacy, but emotional intimacy). If someone wants to experience more intimacy with you, you might respond by sharing more of yourself and your inner feelings, thinking that would create the experience of emotional intimacy.

But really, what creates intimacy is your willingness to be deeply affected by another person. The more you are available to be changed by a person, the more intimacy they are likely to experience with you.

So, if you just allow yourself to be irrevocably changed by those you love—opening yourself to them so much that you will never be the same person again,

Then, you will create deep emotional intimacy with everyone you care about, and you will never be confused about how to create more intimacy when that is what's wanted or needed.

I *Get* To . . . Write and Speak in Clear Story Format

Take the time to write a persuasive piece for your personal or business blog, or in letter to a friend. Use the Clear Story Format below:

You may think that . . .
but really . . .
If you just . . .
Then . . .

Note: I used the Clear Story Format in Chapter 3. See if you can spot it.

24
I'm sorry.
That was my fault.

Never ruin an apology with an excuse.

Unknown

Geez! I've made some stupid mistakes in my life. Where do I begin? Well, I know where I end . . . with many an apology (or with lots of apologies). Some stupid mistakes include:

- Throwing away my boss's good luck charm when I worked at a juice café, thinking it was something someone left and never picked up from lost and found.
- When I was 16, running my car into my parent's metal garage door, busting the brand-new car and my parent's peace of mind.

- The time I let a 1099 contractor go without any previous notice because I was stressed about cash flow and being able to make payroll, leaving her no time at all to plan alternative work.
- The several times I picked up Izzy late from school, which diminished her trust in me as her mom, and, in turn, bruised (or walloped) my self-esteem.

I could continue this list but I am over 40, and I know you don't have all day.

What's important to note is that we all make mistakes. The way I make them right is to face the person and say:

"I am sorry. Is there anything you suggest that will fix the damage that has been done?"

Also . . .

"What you can count on from me moving forward is _____."

The extent of the apology is in direct relation with the mistake. Your hope is the person will forgive and move on, but, in some cases, the indiscretion is so big that it might end the relationship (or require significant time to heal and restore trust). In that case, you will want to take further responsibility and ask the person:

"What can I do to make this right?"

Maybe, you can do nothing at the moment; there is such a thing as apologizing too early. It could come across as insincere or your not having enough time to be present with the gravity of the situation. Gauge it and allow your gut to be your guide. Also, be open to apologizing more than once. It may take more than just one conversation to clear the air.

My friend and team member, Sanyika Calloway, introduced me to the book, *Leadership and Self-Deception* (Berrett-Koehler Publishers, 2015) by The Arbinger Institute. It's a powerful book about how we don't always see ourselves and, therefore, get in our own way and stop the advancement of others—not intentionally, but simply because that's how we're wired.

One particular part of the book focuses on the importance of saying, "I'm sorry," but, more pro-foundly, addresses the feeling and intention behind the words.

To paraphrase, when you say, "I'm sorry," but there is a disconnect between the way you are truly feeling (as if you're not really at fault or shouldn't be the one to have to say "sorry"), it is revealed in your tone and body language and will be noticed above what you say.

We can always tell when we are being tolerated, "put up with," or "put on," and it doesn't feel good because we sense the disingenuousness of the words spoken. If someone senses something other than sincerity within the words you say, the words won't be well received.

Because of this, I am mindful to be present with how I'm feeling and also how the other person perceives the problem or mistake before I apologize. I must admit, there have been times when I've prematurely apologized. I have had to go back and do it again because I wasn't as sincere as I could have been in the original exchange. (Even knowing what I know, this happens more than I'd like to admit with my parents, partner, and especially my teen daughter.)

Another great teacher for me in this area is my business mentor, Victor Cheng. Years ago, he shared his formula for saying sorry with me, and it resonated so well that it's how I've tried to approach apologizing ever since.

He shares that when you make a mistake, do two things:

1) Acknowledge and take responsibility for the mistake
2) Do what you can to rectify the situation.

Cheng shares in his newsletter:

"It's impossible to be perfect 100% of the time. When you make a mistake and take the steps above, you show others two things:

1) You accept personal responsibility for your actions and don't unfairly blame others when you mess up.

2) You're fair to others when you mess up, so it's far more likely you'll be fair when they mess up.

"It's one thing to apologize to your boss when you make a mistake. It's another when you're the boss, and you apologize to your employee."

"In the former, if you don't apologize and make things right, you risk getting fired."

Cheng writes, "In the latter, if you don't apologize, nothing bad happens to you personally. In the short run, you can frankly get away with not acknowledging your mistakes to your direct reports. However, as a leader, the way you handle your own mistakes sets a tone and culture for the way mistakes will be treated in your organization, department, or team."

In a problem-solving culture, admitting you are at fault simply paves the way to focus more on problem prevention. So, the next time you make a mistake, simply say the following:

"I'm sorry. That was my fault. Would you be willing to work with me to figure out how to prevent this problem from happening again in the future?"

This approach works well with direct reports and colleagues.

(It also works well with spouses and your children.)

I *Get* To . . . Apologize

In your journal, share a story from your past that still requires an apology. Then:

1) Acknowledge and take responsibility for the mistake
2) Do what you can to rectify the situation.

25
**There's a line
and, to be clear,
you just crossed it**

*A boundary is only a boundary if you enforce it.
Otherwise, it's just a suggestion.*

Lauren Johnson

From Hollywood to Washington DC to the news media, the #MeToo movement exposed the sexual harassment allegations that for a long time were kept in the dark.

In an article entitled, "Most corporations don't seem worried about a major #MeToo backlash,"

> The explosion of sexual assault allegations did not disrupt Corporate America too much, because many corporations say they already have the proper policies in place. Companies often issue company-wide reminders of policies and procedures. Yet it

is important to note that although Corporations do everything in their power to preclude sexual harassment from occurring, you still get to be prepared with your words if such an event happens. (David Spiegel, "Most corporations don't deem worried about a major #MeToo backlash," December 13, 2017, CNBC Global CFO Council, https://www.cnbc.com/2017/12/13/corporate-america-isnt-concerned-about-a-major-metoo-backlash.html)

The following question was posed on LinkedIn after the #MeToo movement:

"What are you supposed to do when abuse or harassment or inappropriate behavior is starting to happen to you?

"Going forward, in the event someone harasses or acts inappropriately toward me or any other woman (or anybody) in our company, what specifically should I do to respond to nip it in the bud and prevent it from escalating into something that could really hurt people and our company? And also, if I do that, what is it that I can expect as a specific response from the company?"

One woman responded.

"When something inappropriate or invasive happens, I say 'OK: There's a line and, to be clear, you just crossed it. One of two things is going to happen next. Either you apologize to me and assure

me it will never happen again, or I have a conversation with HR or my boss, and they assure me it
will never happen again and tell me the consequences you can expect if you repeat this."

There are a few items that work very well in this
title. The first one I lifted and made it the script of
this chapter.

"There's a line and, to be clear, you just crossed
it." This script is empowering and creates a powerful boundary. It shows the other person that they
crossed a boundary, and it's going to be addressed
in this moment.

In the updated script, it's important to refer
to the *concept* of consequences, but not to use
the *word* consequences. That puts the other person's back against the wall and immediately on
defense. Using threats or extortion, even though
you may have been subjected to it, is not OK,
and will not get the desired result. It's time for
a pattern interruption. Eye for an eye makes the
whole world blind. Coming from compassion is
the next step.

This script goes beyond the #MeToo movement
and is available for anyone to use if they feel an
inappropriate boundary is crossed. If racial discrim-
ination or stereotypes are being flung around the
water cooler or the bathroom stalls, you can pull
from and use this script immediately.

What else works about this script is that the anonymous author gives the other party some options to create a win/win.

There are some items that don't work in this particular scenario. The entire script has an edge to it, which is completely understandable. If your coworker just grabbed you or used a racial slur, it is understandable and even justifiable to have an edge and be pissed, etc., but as I mentioned in the introduction, when you are responding from your critter brain you come from anger and "me against them." The real courage comes from taking a deep breath in and coming from the collective "we."

How I would change it:

"OK: There is a line and, to be clear, you just crossed it. My request is that you apologize to me and assure me it will never happen again. If that is not agreeable to you, I will escalate this situation to HR (or my boss) and they will determine the next action steps. How should we proceed?" Then, listen completely to that person and respond with, "This is too important to have misunderstood a word you said. What I heard you say is (then repeat word for word what they said). Is that correct?"

Wait for them to reply, "Yes," because when they do, that will solidify their commitment.

And if they apologize, state "I accept your apology." For women and men, it is important to write down the date and time of this incident in case the person does this again.

The same script can be used if you hear racial slurs or any other form of verbal harassment . . . whether toward you or someone else. Remember, humans make mistakes. We can hurt others without realizing it. Be open to other people communicating a line that's been crossed from their own perspective.

I *Get* To . . . Be Clear

Write in your journal response to the following prompts:

Has someone said anything inappropriate to you? If so, who and when?

What was your response?

Imagine how the conversation starter, "There's a line and, to be clear, you just crossed it" would have supported you in that situation.

26
**Oh, that's interesting.
I had a different
perspective . . .**

There are no facts, only interpretations.
Friedrich Nietzsche™

Perspective shifting is a skill set I teach in my emotional intelligence and diversity trainings, called Authoring Leadership. It requires listening to other people's perspectives and walking a mile in the other person's shoes. One exercise I use is in the format of story telling. Each participant writes a story from their childhood and describes in detail what it was like growing up from their perspective. They write the story in first-person perspective. Then, everyone folds their individual paper up and hands it in. Then, one by one, they go to the front of the room, pick one of the stories, and read it in the first person. This process creates the opportunity for breakthrough in perspective shifting and overcoming personal biases.

Asserting your perspective

How do you express your opinion, perspectives, or ideas while respecting those senior to you?

Victor Cheng has a strategy to do so using the following communication script: "Oh, that's interesting. I had a different perspective on the issue, and a different approach in mind."

By allowing them the space to decide for themselves, you're non-verbally stating: "I respect your position, authority, and decision-making role in this situation. I am not trying to challenge your power. I simply have additional information for *you* to consider."

I *Get* To . . . Have a Different Perspective

In your team or group, re-create the perspective-shifting exercise above.

27
What I heard you say is . . .

One of the most sincere forms of respect is
actually listening to what another has to say.
Bryant H. McGill

Everyone wants to be seen and heard. I believe that human conflict derives from one, both, or all parties feeling they weren't seen or heard.

In the early days of my business, I lacked basic customer service skills. I didn't want to hear any complaint or feedback. I walled off myself to what people were saying and either delegated or ignored the very constructive feedback I received from my clients—and could have put into practice if I had just listened. More often that not, these folks just wanted to help and see my business and me succeed.

Since 2013, customer service has been the favorite part of my business. I absolutely find joy in connecting with people. In my customer engagement, I will say the following sentence starter to communicate back what I heard them say: "What I heard you say is . . ."

This makes people feel seen and heard, and I acknowledge them and welcome their feedback as I have amazing customers who want to send referrals my way.

Kelly Morgan, a client and a fabulous writing coach, says "One of things I also did while teaching is to slow down communication and listen for feelings and needs . . . repeat what I heard, ask questions . . . rather than give advice. When people feel heard, I learned there is so much more harmony and compassion."

Simply repeat

Social skills expert and author, Leil Lowndes, recommends simple repetition. In *How to Talk to Anyone: 92 Little Tricks for Big Success in Relationships* (McGraw Hill, 1999), Lowndes writes to "simply repeat—or parrot—the last two or three words your companion said, in a sympathetic, questioning tone. That throws the conversational ball right back in your partner's court. It shows you're listening, interested, and lets them get back to telling their story. You've got to be slightly savvy about this one, but it's surprisingly effective. Surprisingly effective? Yes, it is. It is?"

Intonation is key here again, I don't recommend sounding like a parrot. You want to be genuine and authentic in your tone and words.

I *Get* To . . . Listen

For a 24-hour period, listen. Just listen. Then, after someone talks with you, follow up with, "What I heard you say is . . .".

28
What do you mean by that?

The important thing is not to stop questioning.
Curiosity has its own reason for existing.
Albert Einstein

When my mentor Victor Cheng went to Stanford, he took five courses that have been the most useful to him during his 20-year career. Those classes were:

1. Introduction to Economics
2. Social Psychology
3. Statistics
4. Public Speaking
5. Peer Counseling

He feels the most surprising class on that list is peer counseling. The premise of the class was to train to be a peer counselor for the on-campus suicide prevention hotline.

Cheng shares, "In peer counseling, I learned to communicate in emotionally high-stakes situations by learning to listen . . . really listen . . . to another person without judgment."

He adds that the class was not intended for psychotherapy professionals, so they we were not allowed to give any advice. Rather, all students taught to do was to listen and ask clarifying questions.

He adds, "It never ceases to amaze me how much you can learn about and connect with another person by truly paying attention to them."

Clarifying questions help us to better understand what has been said in a conversation. The questions allow you to go narrow and deeper and learn the intent behind what is being said. Additionally, they slow down the conversation.

"Questions trigger a mental reflex known as 'instinctive elaboration.' When a question is posed, it takes over the brain's thought process." David Hoffeld writes, "And when your brain is thinking about the answer to a question, it can't contemplate anything else." That's why question-asking plays a role in suicide prevention." (https://www.fastcompany.com/3068341/want-to-know-what-your-brain-does-when-it-hears-a-question)

Some examples of clarifying questions include:

- What do you mean by that?
- Can you give me an example of a situation that reflects your concern?
- If that issue were handled better, what would it have looked like instead?
- What do you mean by "you're upset?"
- What happened?
- How did you feel about what happened?
- What are your thoughts when you are frustrated?
- How do you experience overwhelm?

Tone of clarifying questions

Remember, the tone of your voice impacts how your questions are received. "What do you mean by that?" although a clarifying question, could come off as confrontational if said the "wrong" way. Whereas "Tell me more about that" invites the other person to semantically join the sentence with you. Amy Rutt, a LinkedIn colleague, who suggested this phrase says, "My purpose is to deepen my understanding so that I know how I can have impact."

Questions require a safe delivery to get the desired result. A "safe delivery" is a warm and compassionate delivery . . . with an intonation that creates invitation not fear. Adding "I'm curious . . ." before "What do you mean by that?" can soften the delivery. Using "I'm curious" with your clarifying questions positions you in a place of curiosity rather than interrogation. Taking a deep breath and softening your expression and tone before asking questions can support you in safe delivery.

Personally, this has been an area of growth for me. I have received feedback that my delivery can be curt, direct, or intense when I ask questions. "You sometimes talk at people vs. with people" is feedback I've received. Of course, it's difficult to hear this feedback, and I reframe it by thinking, "This person is committed to making me better."

What people say vs. what they mean

Because Victor Cheng took those five courses in college, he recognizes that listening skills are paramount in business and in life. He states, "During my many role-playing practice sessions, I came to appreciate that what people say versus what they mean aren't always the same thing. People in crisis aren't always the most precise in their communication." Indeed, people in crisis or perceived crisis ("This feedback feels like an attack") can be triggered by your clarifying questions.

The greater lesson: When somebody says something, don't react immediately. Take a pause

(Chapter 22). Also, understand that, whether in crisis or perceived crisis, what someone says versus what they mean may not be the same thing.

Self-directed clarifying questions

Whenever I am challenged by a certain event or circumstance, or triggered by a comment from a family member or friend, I ask *myself* the following clarifying questions:

- What are my thoughts?
- What are my feelings?
- What are my physical sensations?

Let's examine each one.

What are my thoughts? (Mind)

I have thoughts of (fill in the blank).

Some thoughts are fleeting, whereas some are all consuming.

"Every problem starts with a thought. We think a certain way about something, and by sticking with that thought and giving it importance, we create misery for ourselves. Being present gives us the possibility to see the thought just as a thought and not identify with it." (*Freedom is in this Moment*, Breema Center Publishing, 2004)

Have you ever obsessed over a thought? Perhaps over a person whom did you wrong?

You might think: "Mr. So-n-So did me wrong." Cancel, cancel . . . and change that to:

"I have thoughts of Mr. So-n-So doing me wrong."

See the difference? Recognize your thought as a thought that is separate from you (you are not your thoughts), as exemplified in the following example.

OMG. I didn't get enough sleep. I'm not prepared for this. I should've stayed home last night and practiced. What am I going to do to get through this? This is so bad. When will I ever learn? OMG.

vs.

I have thoughts that I am not prepared for this presentation to the board.

What are my feelings? (Heart)

I have feelings of (fill in the blank).

There are four basic human emotions: Anger, Sadness, Fear, and Happiness. These are the primal emotions of human beings.

If you "feel disappointed" or "feel excited" or "feel tired," those aren't emotions. They could be a culmination of a lot of negative thoughts. "I have thoughts of disappointment" or "I have thoughts of feeling tired." My aim to share these sentence starters is not to make you sound like a robot, because these can feel quite counterintuitive in terms of how we have been communicating our feelings our entire life. However, I want you to understand that you are not your feelings any more than you are your thoughts.

These are the four ways to express emotions:

I have feelings of anger, or I feel angry.

I have feelings of sadness, or I feel sad,

I have feelings of fear, or I feel fearful.

I have feelings of happiness, or I feel happy.

According to this school of thought (pun intended), you can only feel these four emotions (or some derivative thereof), and the rest are thoughts.

What are my physical sensations? (Body)

I have physical sensations of (fill in the blank), such as:

I have physical sensations of my heart racing.

I have physical sensations of my chest clenching.

I have physical sensations of my shoulders dropping.

I have physical sensations of sweaty palms.

I have physical sensations of shortness of breath.

I have physical sensations of the hairs standing up on the back of my neck.

I have physical sensations of a lump in my throat.

So what do you do with all these answers to your self-directed clarifying questions? This is an exercise in awareness. The more aware you become of the thoughts, feelings, and physical sensations you are having, the easier it will be to assess and address. You can notice what's happening to you; think about what your mind, heart, and body are communicating to you; and do you what you need to do to become more grounded again.

I *Get* To . . . Question

During this experiential exercise, I invite you to slow down. In your next significant communication, go slow by asking more clarifying questions. Think a second or two longer before you speak. Journal the answers to these questions.

- How does your partner respond to your clarifying questions?
- How do you respond to your self-directed clarifying questions?

29
My truth in this moment . . .

No legacy is so rich as honesty.
William Shakespeare

"My truth in this moment" is both a response and my lead-in during difficult conversations or sharing intimate or emotional matters. This conversation starter is a way to instantly ground and drop into your heart. The words, and the energy behind them, transfix the other and calls for pause and attention. When you express your truth, you reach a level of awareness, acknowledgement, and acceptance before you begin speaking.

It's an opening to vulnerability.

Like this: My truth in this moment is this is the chapter I've been dreading to write. Why? I felt very exposed when I wrote my first book and the media tour that followed. My first book I published was written to a 20- to 30-year-old female audience, and it was a book that was *Sex and The City* meets *Think and Grow Rich.* Since the book you are reading is meant for those interested in business, leadership, and communications, I did not want to mention my old book—for several reasons, but I will reveal my truth later in this chapter.

First, let's discuss the dictionary definition of vulnerability: To be susceptible to physical or emotional attack or harm. Synonyms include helpless, defenseless, powerless, impotent, weak, and susceptible.

No wonder people think being vulnerable is weak.

To me, vulnerability is strength. My definition of vulnerability is to tear down the walls around your heart and to let others in. When you are vulnerable, you are open, disarmed, and ready to create intimacy and go deep with others.

Relationships are about relating. No better way to relate than to be vulnerable. By sharing your truth or telling your story, you create common ground with others. If you walk around like a badass with a steel heart and ego to match, others will never get to know the real you. Heck, *you* won't know the real you.

When it comes to relationships, the only way to develop intimacy is to tear down the ways we protect our hearts and be open to share our truth. No better way than to use the words "My truth in this moment . . ." because it is a really powerful preface to speak what's truly going on with you. Again, this type of statement requires a breath—a meditative moment to really go deep to discuss what your truth in this moment really is.

My truth broadcasted

I mentioned in the introduction that I was "thrown under a bus" by a financial journalist when my first book came out.

"Thrown under a bus" is such victim language. If anything, I threw *myself* under a bus.

My book, *Goal Digger: Lessons Learned from the Rich Men I Dated,* was a self-help book intended to share lessons I learned from dating wealthy men. I started writing the book when I was 29. I self-published it when I was 31.

I have told this story on so many occasions, and I actually *still* feel very vulnerable sharing it here, because this book is a communications book. I want you, the reader, to think of me as a leader and not that "nasty" name Jean Chatzsky called me that day.

I remember it distinctly. It was a fall day in New York City in 2007. When I entered the Time Warner building I was so excited . . . I felt I had arrived. I mean, every new author wants to get on Oprah, and Oprah and Friends Radio was the next best thing. Jean Chatzky, a respected financial journalist, didn't give me the friendliest of welcomes when I entered the radio studio, but I wrote off the weird energetic exchange to nerves.

When she started the interview, she asked me the standard questions, including: "Why did you write the book? Are you a millionaire yet? Did you only date these men for money?" The answer was "no" to the last two questions . . . it was indeed a book to share the success habits of wealthy men and how women can do it, too.

And then she asked me a completely valid question that caught me off guard, but that I answered honestly.

She asked, "Did any of these men give you money?"

I was so naive. I wasn't prepared for this question. My publicist did not prepare me for this question. Without a pause I answered, "Yes."

She then uncrossed and crossed her other leg, and said "Hmmmmm . . . you sound like a *working girl* to me."

Silence.

I was a deer in headlights. Did she really just say that? On radio, OMG. You've got to be kidding me?

Instantly I dimmed my light.

To tell you the truth, my explanation was that I dated a man for a year, and he wanted me to travel with him internationally. I said I couldn't because I have my business and daughter, and he simply said, "Let me help you out."

Too long for a sound byte. Too short to retain my dignity.

I walked out of the Oprah and Friends studio, dejected.

I was committed to that never happening again.

It was also the last time I actively promoted my book to the media. And, I must admit, I have been gun-shy to be in the interviewee seat ever since.

Did it happen to me or did it happen for me?

My truth in this moment is that was a beautiful lesson in forgiveness—forgiving others and myself. Her comment propelled me in another direction, and I am thankful that I have been able to share my experience and my talent to support thousands in sharing their voice and message in the world.

I *Get* To . . . Be Vulnerable

During your next significant conversation at home or work, share what your truth is in this moment. Open up and be vulnerable and share your soul. This will deepen the relationships at home and work and will also create common ground between you and others. When you open your heart, you allow others to do the same. If this feels raw for you now, I invite you to share the "My truth in this moment is . . ." while gazing into a mirror.

Some examples: You're having an intense conversation with your mother, "My truth in this moment is . . . I am scared to share with you some of my most intimate thoughts for feeling of being judged."

Your boss is raising her voice to you, "My truth in this moment is . . . I do not feel comfortable with the way that you're treating me."

30
I need a moment . . .

*The meeting of two eternities . . . the past and
future . . . is precisely the present moment.*
Henry David Thoreau

I used to be a badass without tact and would
often bulldoze people. Yet, I did a lot of work
in "feminine leadership" and started to see that I
could be in my power without being forceful or
aggressive, really leaning into grace, ease, and
trusting the process.

Once, I asked a friend for advice on how to handle a matter in my life where I felt like *I* was the
one being bulldozed.

She said, tell him, "I need you to stop talking,
don't say another word. Keep that shit to yourself, I

don't want to hear this now or ever. Go share with your other friends."

For some reason, this script didn't land for me. It was powerful when it came out of her mouth. The critter brain Alicia was thinking, "Yeah baby, and at the end of shouting that, I'm going to kick open a door to make my exit."

The intelligent brain Alicia was thinking it wasn't totally kind, and there's a better way. I mean, if you are in a heated conversation with someone and respond in that way, it will only incite the other party to make things worse.

Instead, try the following script. This script works well for interpersonal conflicts with spouses and partners.

If you and your spouse are in an argument and one party tosses a low blow, take three breaths in and out. (Remember the pause?)

Instead of blowing up and telling them to SHUT THE F*** up, say the following:

"I need a moment. I am processing what you are saying and would like a moment to think. Can we reconnect later today to discuss?"

Or, you can try the following script:

"Thank you for sharing (thoughts/feelings/physical sensations). I need some time to process. Can we discuss after the kids go to bed?"

These scripts give you time to process—you are responding versus reacting. Also, you are giving the other person time to process, too. This diffuses the situation and gives you the opportunity to step away.

Many of you may wonder what to say when you come back together later. Did you just delay the inevitable?

Try this . . .

"I thought about our previous discussion, and it's important to me that we come to a positive conclusion. I want to acknowledge you for sharing your feelings and my experience is (fill in the blank). What can we do to move past this?

Or . . .

My truth in this moment is that what you said was hurtful. I want us to come together to heal what has been hurt.

I *Get* To . . . Have a Moment

Write in your journal a response to this prompt: How can verbally requesting a moment shift you from reaction to response?

31

_____

people _____
people

Loving people live in a loving world. Hostile people live in a hostile world. Same world.

Wayne W. Dyer

Hurt people hurt people.
 Connected people connect with people.
Angry people anger people.
Respectful people respect people.

_____ people _____ people.
(Fill in the blanks.)

These aren't really conversation starters, but they're opportunities for increasing awareness when understanding the intricacies of human behavior.

We all come with some sort of baggage, hurt, traumas, misunderstanding, and, if we don't, we know someone who does. My invitation is that we stop the ripple effect by changing our way of being and what we create in the world. We all create our own reality, and if we don't heal our own personal traumas, then what we do is perpetuate destructive behavior.

For example, "Hurt people hurt people." If someone is hurting you, intentionally or not, run this script through your head to realize they have been hurt themselves. Through compassion, we can shift the script.

"Loving people love people"

How can you impact the person's life that was hurtful to you? I contend loving them is the best solution. And, finally, healed people heal people. Your giveback to the world will be creating conversations of love, connection, and compassion.

Life is a ripple effect. What is your contribution?

I *Get* To . . . Love

Consider the example of "Hurt people hurt people." When someone hurts you, here are some questions to reflect on:

- What's happening in their life that made them say that to you?
- What would it look like to walk a mile in their shoes?
- How can you respond to stop the cycle?

32
What would it look like?

In order to carry a positive action we must develop here a positive vision.

Dalai Lama

If you haven't figured out already, visualization is my secret weapon. There is power in focusing on *source* energy through practices like creative visualization, affirmations, vision boarding, and creating as you speak. Now, I really don't want to lose the corporate people, because I'm really not that woo-woo, I'm a workhorse that drives a BMW, but I can firmly tell you this: I create the life I want by visualizing first.

In 1997, I traveled to Costa Rica with my best friend, Melissa, who is quoted in this book, and we wrote in a journal what we wanted from our life. I distinctly remember it to this day: I want to be my own boss, get paid for what I know, not what I do, and travel . . . a lot. Voilà, I have accomplished it and then some, and it doesn't stop there. Regularly, I up level my game, by asking my team, my clients, and myself:

"What would it look like?"

What would it look life if . . .

Perhaps you've pondered questions about changes you desire to make in your life. And maybe you've even asked them out loud to your team members, colleagues, and family members.

What would your life look like if you started working out daily—whether to achieve a particular weight loss goal or as a shifted lifestyle commitment?

What would it look like if we worked collaboratively as a team by brainstorming best practices during an ongoing product launch instead of at the conclusion of the project?

What would it look like if . . .

- I faced my fears about ____?
- I confronted my sister-in-law about ___?
- I asked for a raise?
- I took the sabbatical from work?
- I started a business?

In my coaching and training business, this is a question I pose for others to induce imagination and creativity.

What would it look like if it were easy?
What would it look like if you could follow your dreams *and* make a living?

My 16-year-old daughter, Izzy, continues to be a great teacher for me and I am so pleased that I get to use this technique with her as she creates a life that she desires.

Universal law is powerful and it works when applied. These may seem like "soft skills," or non-tangibles, but I have used the power of this process to make strides in my business and life that are remarkable, even to me.

What I know for sure is it's a beautiful gift to get to ask this question of yourself, your children, your spouse or partner, your team—your life.

I *Get* To . . . Look

Write five of your own "what would it look like" scenarios and take the time to journal your thoughtful responses.

33
I'm curious . . .

Curiosity will conquer fear even more than bravery will.

James Stephens

I was in a conversation with a gentleman who was born in New Delhi, India, and raised in Manchester, England. He was sharing his perspective of both cultures in terms of communication and connectedness, and said jokingly, "When someone boards a bus in India and the bus is pretty much empty, except for one lone passenger, the person boarding would not only sit next to the other person, but very close to that person (what westerners might feel would be invading personal space). He continued, "In England, the person boarding the bus would sit as far away as possible from the other passenger."

We giggled over our shared experience, as I've been to India three times and to England more times than I can count.

I shared my personal story of traveling across India by train on the "3rd Class Sleeper," from Varanasi to Pune. There is a reason I mention "3rd Class." In India, with their historic caste system, that is probably the worst way to travel, but for me it was a wildly colorful, suspenseful, and "off the beaten track" experience that included goats, dogs, crying babies, and a "bathroom" that was a hole in the floor of the train with views of the train tracks.

When I was on the train, I purchased my own "berth" or bed, but throughout the 20- to 24-hour journey, plenty of people joined me in my bed. I even got my feet massaged a few times (unwillingly). Anyway, on the journey, there were various people sitting on the bed above mine, and I swear they would stare at me their entire journey. One guy was leaning over the rail for 2+ hours. I shared this story with the man, and he laughed, and said "That's Indians for you. We are a curious people. They were probably in awe with you."

Curiosity is a beautiful human space. While I'm not telling you to sit up close to someone, stare, or massage someone's feet without asking, I do encourage you to be curious in your communication.

When you come from a space of curiosity, you create a safe and non-judgmental space for others to share. And when you express your own genuine, child-like curiosity, it deepens your learning, empathy and relationships with others.

Curiosity is a win/win opportunity.

When you use the conversation starter, "I'm curious" usually before a sentence like, "What was your experience of that?" . . . not only is it a softer delivery, you also turn on the curiosity receptor in your brain, which leads to "Three benefits of curiosity."

Three benefits of curiosity

1) **Deeper learning:** "Curiosity may put the brain in a state that allows it to learn and retain any kind of information, like a vortex that sucks in what you are motivated to learn, and also everything around it," says Dr. Matthias Gruber, lead author of the cognitive neuroscience study from the University of California, Davis. (Andoree Durayappah-Harrison MAPP, "The Secret Benefits of a Curious Mind," October 8, 2014, https://www.psychologytoday.com/us/blog/thriving101/201410/the-secret-benefits-curious-mind)

2) **Deeper relationships:** As you ask questions and are curious about other people, not only do you learn more . . . you also deepen

the relationship and create connection. "One study asked strangers to pose and answer personal questions, a process scientists call 'reciprocal self-disclosure.' They found that people were rated as warmer and more attractive if they showed real curiosity in the exchange (while other variables like the person's social anxiety and their levels of positive and negative emotions did not affect the partner's feelings of attraction and closeness). This implies that demonstrating curiosity toward someone is a great way to build your closeness with them." (Emily Campbell, "Six Surprising Benefits of Curiosity," MindBody, GreaterGoodMagazine.com, September 24, 2015, https://greatergood.berkeley.edu/article/item/six_surprising_benefits_of_curiosity)

3) **Deeper happiness:** I love to share the aphorism, "When in doubt, focus out." When you focus on others, not only do you learn more and create connection, but you are happier. Thinking about ourselves all the time is the fastest way to self-scrutiny and thoughts of depression. In the same article by Emily Campbell, she writes, "Research has shown curiosity to be associated with higher levels of positive emotions, lower levels of anxiety, more satisfaction with life, and greater psychological well-being."

I *Get* To . . . Be Curious

Schedule a lunch or coffee with a new friend . . . someone you don't know every well. Really get curious about them in the conversation. Focus on spending most of the conversation on asking clarifying questions (Chapter 28). Then journal, what did you learn about them from that conversation? What did you learn about yourself?

**34
What is
something you're
excited about?**

*You never get a second chance to make a first
impression.*

Unknown

A s Americans, asking "What do you do?" swiftly
comes out of our mouths at networking events
when what we actually desire is to go deeper
and discuss something more substantial. In other
continents such as Europe, asking "What do you
do?" is considered rude.

Why not move from perceived "etiquette" to creating a more memorable connection by using more
significant and interesting questions.

Ice breakers and mingle mixers

Consider asking these conversation-starting questions at your next social gathering or networking event:

- What is something you're excited about?
- What is something you learned today?
- How did your first job help you get where you are?
- Tell us about a time you blew someone away?
- How do you spend most of your time?

I *Get* To . . . Connect

Always wanted to know about the people you've met, but didn't think to ask? Make the list of conversation-starting questions here or in your journal.

35
I need your support

*A man's pride can be his downfall, and he
needs to learn when to turn to others for
support and guidance.*

Bear Grylls

"I need your support." I say this to my daughter all
the time when I feel the power dynamics are off,
and I am stretching for new ways to communicate.
When my daughter was younger, it was obvious I
was in charge. Now that she is a teenager, we have
an alpha female dynamic in the house, yet, I am
still in charge . . . it's just not so obvious to her (and
sometimes, *me*). I use intentional communication
to create space for her to individuate and express

defiance, and I maintain my authority. Let me tell you this, it's a delicate dance.

I see that she wants to dominate me, and one way I support her if we are butting heads on a contentious subject is I will say, "I need your support." It's disarming. I become the gentle puppy that rolls over on their back, and she becomes the dominant that can save her poor mommy who just turned into a puppy. Christine Comaford has called this the "dom-sub swap," and says, "When the dominant person uses it, they enroll and engage the subordinate person resulting in a temporary transfer of power. This is especially effective when you want a person to change their behavior or take on more responsibility."

Masculine - Feminine swap

I also use "dom-sub swap" in my relationship with my hubby. As an alpha female in a relationship with an alpha male, to get what I want, I ground into my feminine. What the heck does that mean? Well there are entire books on this subject, I suggest *The Way of the Superior Man* by David Dieda (1997). To give you context here, just as there is a dom-sub dynamic in play in a variety of situations (like with my daughter or in corporate settings), there is a masculine and feminine dynamic in every relationship (both homosexual and heterosexual relationships). Again, see David Dieda for more on this subject.

When my hubby and I were driving through Eastern Europe one summer, he, as a former stunt driver, was driving through the highways and byways of Albania and Macedonia like a bat out of hell. I was white knuckling our way through mountainous switchbacks on our way to Montenegro at 120 mph, and my dominant masculine side, and my amygdala, and my alpha female all in chorus wanted to scream, "SLOW THE %&*# DOWN!"

Now, if I did yell expletives and attempted to dominate the situation, I know there would have been a power struggle, which would have triggered his amygdala. It would have been a lose/lose battle.

Instead I breathed, dug deep, leaned into my feminine, and softly said "Babe, when you drive fast it makes me feel unsafe, can you make me feel safe again?"

He smiled warmly, and said in his Dutch accent, "Certainly, darling." And he slowed down the car to a comfortable pace of 80 mph.

I *Get* To . . . Receive Support

Are you someone who does everything themselves? Would you like some support? For the
next seven days, ask for support at least once a
day (e.g., support with taking the groceries from
your car or having someone fuel your gas tank
or asking your partner for a foot massage). This
may feel like a stretch for those who like to do
everything themselves but remember . . . asking
for support gives the person you are asking an
increase in their happy hormones. Win/win.

36
Would it be of support if . . .

The purpose of human life is to serve, and to show compassion and the will to help others.
Albert Schweitzer

L ife is not a solo act. Just as we learned in the last chapter, we need support, but sometimes people are not comfortable asking for it. Either they have feelings of unworthiness or intense pride (which can just be a mask for unworthiness). As 21st century humans, we are under continuous stress and distress, so using the conversation starter, "Would it be of support if . . ." is a great way to support people in calming their nervous systems. The extra benefit? By doing so, you help yourself.

In her article, "The Neuroscience of Giving," Eva Ritvo M.D., writes: "Helping others can take on many forms. Small repeated boosts of the Happiness Trifecta (dopamine, serotonin, and oxytocin) will produce the most benefit so find ways to give and to give often." (Eva Ritvo M.D., "The Neuroscience of Giving," www.psychologytoday.com, April 24, 2014, https://www.psychologytoday.com/us/blog/vitality/201404/the-neuroscience-giving)

Here are some ways to give support:

At work: "I know you have been having a lot of personal issues at home. Would it be of support if we order lunch in to help you complete your report by your deadline?"

To your stressed teenager: "Love, I know you are very stressed with finals, and you are working extremely hard. Would be of support if I organize and clean your room this week, and you can take that responsibility back on after your finals?"

To your spouse/partner: "Babe, I know you have been working hard on your feet at the salon all week. Would it be of support if I gave you a long foot rub and made dinner for the kids tonight?"

I *Get* To . . . Support

When someone is struggling, when you energetically experience them being in fight/flight/freeze, use this phrase to offer a solution, "Would it be of support if . . .?" This will help them shift focus from the problem to a course of action or positive outcome.

How did this make them feel? How did it make you feel?

37
What can we do to ...? Because when we do, we will ...

Alone we can do so little; together we can do so much.

Helen Keller

At the California Women's Conference, I was in a conversation with two female aerospace engineers who complained to me about the pay inequity in their company and how they felt disempowered because they were not being paid equally to their male counterparts. I suggested they go to Human Resources to discuss. They asked me what they should say. That's when I enrolled the support of my mentor Dr. Mark Goulston, who is a bestselling author of *Just Listen* and medical psychiatrist. He suggested the following communication script:

"What can we do to bridge the pay gap between men and women at our organization? Because when we do we will attract the top talent, increase employee morale and it will create great PR for our company."

I call this a "Partnering from the Start" script. When you partner with the other party, whether it's another person or organization, and use the inclusive pronoun "we" instead of using tribal distinction of "us" against "them," you create a partnership to focus on a collective solution that will have collective benefits.

What could we accomplish using the "collective we"?

From LinkedIn to Facebook, folks on social media loved this script, and wanted more. I love this exchange between my client Diane Beck and Dr. Mark Goulston.

Diane Beck This is great! I love the scripted question by Dr. Goulston. I'm also really curious of scripted "counters" to the anticipated responses from HR that would lead to the pay raise.

Mark Goulston. Try this with HR and/or CEO's after you're an absolute good sport about your next compensation conversation (if it's meager they'll be prepared for you to complain or look hurt, etc. So, when you're gracious—when they wouldn't be—it can be disarming). Ask to meet with them on the day after and say: "Going forward, what do I need to get done for the company and you, for you to 'champion' and go to bat for my getting the biggest pay raise and promotion when I am next reviewed?" Graciously push them to get granular and then say, "This is too important for me to not be totally clear on what you will need to see to go to bat and champion me when I am next up for a raise and promotion. So, what I heard you say is _____ (repeat exactly what they said). Is that correct?" Wait for a confirmatory "Yes" to cause them to deepen their commitment to going to bat and championing you. Then finish by saying, "And since this is so important to me, I will plan on checking in with you every couple of months to see if I am on track with what I need to get done and/or if I need to make a course correction. What's the best way for me to schedule that?"

Here's the script:

"What can we do to (SOLVE SAID PROBLEM)? Because when we do, we will (RECEIVE THE FOLLOWING BENEFITS)."

I *Get* To . . . Write

During the writing exercises, how can you partner from the start with a colleague or organization? Perhaps you want to start an initiative, solve a problem, or lead a team with a new project. Use the following script to create change and opportunity:

What can we do to (SOLVE SAID PROBLEM)? Because when we do, we will (RECEIVE THE FOLLOWING BENEFITS).

38
I invite you . . .

Nothing annoys people so much as not receiving invitations.

Oscar Wilde

Everyone likes an invitation. I personally use "I invite you" in my coaching practice as an alternative to "You should . . ." or "I challenge you." I also use this language as a counterbalance to scary, out-of-my-comfort-zone tasks.

During my book writing workshops, when we get to the part where authors start pre-marketing their books and doing some market research with their readers, I will usually state:

"This is the part of the day that I invite you to use Facebook LIVE to connect with your audience."

or

"I invite you to do a Facebook LIVE and announce the book you are writing and request feedback."

No, that is not scary at all! (Okay, it's a bit scary, but that's your critter brain objecting on behalf of your comfort zone.) This is when the "extroverts" or more "social media driven" authors in the room get out their smartphones and start getting ready for their videos. Usually the camera-shy folks make it happen because of the group dynamic and by seeing it role modeled by their not-so-camera-shy fellow participants. So, it's more of an "experience" invitation.

Permission-based invites

Keep in mind, as a coach, I ask permission of my clients to take a stand for them and invite them into new ways of being. Personal growth requires stretching outside of our comfort zones. So when you stand for your client and a new level of growth, you want to invite them to take action.

I love invitations, too! One of my mantras is "Alicia attracts invitations, recognition, and opportunity."

Anatomy of an invite

First, you want to acknowledge the person and recognize them for their willingness to grow and learn. Second, you want to invite them to an exciting new challenge and/or event. And finally, just for fun and not all the time, I ask with a smile, "Do you accept my invitation?"

1) Acknowledge
2) Invite
3) Do you accept my invitation? (Optional)

I *Get* To . . . Invite

During this exercise, think of your friends and family, and write an "Invitation list." Perhaps invite them to opportunities for personal growth.

Name: _____ I invite you to _____
_____

Name: _____ I invite you to _____
_____

Name: _____ I invite you to _____
_____

39
Imagine . . .

If you can dream it, you can do it.
Walt Disney

During my workshops, seminars, and events, I often hold space for closed-eye visualization exercises. Recently, I was teaching a workshop on "Overcoming Overwhelm," and I had the 30 participants close their eyes and visualize their ideal 24 hours.

I spoke into the space, "Imagine you are the director of your own movie and the star of the show. Describe in detail your ideal day, such as:

- What would your ideal 24 hours look like?
- Who do you wake up next to?
- Who greets you in the morning?

- What are the sights and smells of the environment?
- What are you creating that day?
- Who is the last person you say goodnight to before you fall into slumber?"

Imagine if you are an artist, and you start every morning with a blank canvas. Well, that's what is available to all of us. In the game called life, your *mind* must arrive at a destination before your *life* does.

David Hoffeld, author of *The Science of Selling,* shares in *Fast Company* magazine that "research has found that the more the brain contemplates a behavior, the more likely it is that we will engage in it. [. . .] Just thinking about doing something can shift your perception and even alter your body chemistry."

That's why imagination is so important—if you spend all your time focusing on right-now realities, the consciousness of effects, or what you need to do (such as balancing your checking account, paying your bills, meeting your deadlines for projects, etc.), then you are not focusing your energy on *source*—the imagination that has endless supply. Imagination flows freely with no limits. Don't limit life by your current results. Lean in and imagine your true desires.

Derek Sivers, founder of CD Baby, says "If we love something, it seems easy. We imagine it as one fun step."

I was fascinated by his audiobook *Anything You Want: 40 Lessons for A New Kind of Entrepreneur* (Portfolio, 2015) and the creativity and risk-taking he openly shared. In his blog, he posts:

> People often ask me about starting my company. 'It must have been so difficult! That's a huge undertaking! How did you manage all of that?' But I just answer sincerely, "There was really nothing to it. I just made this little website, and people liked it. That's it." I barely even remember the details. In my head it was just one fun step. Now I have to pay attention to that, with each new project I start. How many steps am I imagining?

Whether a closed-eye visualization, or a vision board party amongst friends, creating the life you want starts with imagining, and imagining yourself enjoying the journey.

Imagine . . .

I highly recommend the book, *Words that Work* (Hachette Books, 2008) by Dr. Frank Luntz. In it, he includes the word "Imagine" in his list of "Words and Phrases for the Twenty-First Century."

He states, "'Imagine' is one of the most powerful words in the English language. [. . .] The word 'imagine' is an open, non-restrictive command—almost an invitation. Its power is derived from the simple fact that it can conjure up anything in the mind of the one doing the imagining."

Imagination and visualization are synonymous in their meanings to create a mental picture. After you create the mental picture, you manifest your desired results. Or you reverse engineer. Even the book you are reading now began as a mental image. I used my own book writing strategy as an incubator to create the words you are reading on this very page. Every detail was a mental image. And now, my reality matches my imagination.

Imagination at work

In a corporate setting, when you are requesting a raise, you want to evoke imagination in your boss or the decision maker. As Dr. Frank Luntz further shares in his book, *Words that Work*:

> "'*Imagine if . . .*' are the two most effective words you can use in this situation. '*Imagine if* I hadn't been here to work on Project X.' '*Imagine if* Contract Y hadn't been hammered out last week.' By merely inviting your boss to do a little thought experiment, you prompt a subtle but clear vision of you being out of the picture if more money isn't in your future. And if you achieve the "imagine if" visualization by demonstrating your *future* value, chances are you'll end up getting that raise, bonus or promotion."

Imagination turns present propositions into future value, impossible feats into possible realities, and obstacles into opportunities.

When you imagine, you tap into creative and spiritual source and surpass your mere mortal skills.

I *Get* To . . . Imagine

During the visualization exercise, imagine where you will be one year from now. Write your visualizations in the categories below.

Personal: _____

Career: _____

Health: _____

Romance: _____

40
If you remember only one thing, remember this . . .

The true art of memory is the art of attention.
Samuel Johnson

It's easy to get lost in checking out YouTube land, watching TEDx videos, and listening to bootlegged audiobooks. While doing this myself, that's when I stumbled upon videos of Dr. Frank Luntz, the corporate communications expert and Republican strategist I introduced in the last chapter. During a keynote, he confidently set up the following sentence starter:

"If you remember only one thing, remember this . . ."

This simple set-up will direct your audience to remember one thing and one thing only . . . the words you mention after that statement.

Fair enough. It definitely got my attention.

As E.E. Cummings grabbed my attention with this share:

> . . . *remember one thing only:* that it's you—nobody else—who determines your destiny and decides your fate. Nobody else can be alive for you; nor can you be alive for anybody else.

When to use?

That's a good question. What is the best time, situation, or circumstance to use this phrase:

> "If you remember only one thing, remember this . . ."?

My suggestion is to use this sentence starter at the end of a keynote, TEDx talk, webinar, or business address. You would use this when addressing a group as opposed to one person, as it's more of a broadcast than an intimate share.

Yet, when it comes to the business address, Victor Cheng says the phrasing feels a tad bit aggressive. "It's set up as a command. I would soften it a hair."

Depending on the audience, Cheng advises this alteration: "If you remember only one thing from *this talk*, my hope is you will remember this . . ." The reason why: In the case when the audience is comprised of leaders senior to his authority, Cheng wouldn't want to inadvertently challenge the hierarchy by sounding commanding. So, to avoid the power dynamic, that's the change he would make.

I *Get* To . . . Remember One Thing Only

That was fast. You are almost done with the book. So far, what has landed for you? In this brainstorming exercise, list the insights you remember so far. From the list, circle the ONE THING that stands out. Then post it on social media with #IGetTo, and tag me @aliciadunams.

_____

_____

_____

_____

_____

_____

_____

_____

_____

_____

_____

_____

_____

_____

_____

BONUS Now, It's Your Turn . . .

Tell me, how has the way you connect in conversation changed your relationships and life?

What do you use as conversation starters to create deeper and more meaningful communication with your friends, family, and colleagues?

Please share them below and also use social media to Tweet, Instagram, and Facebook your conversation starters with #IGetTo, and tag me @ aliciadunams.

And if you share a screenshot by emailing it IGetTo@aliciadunams.com, we will enter you in a drawing to feature your submission in the next edition of my next "I Get To" book series.

I *Get* To . . . Share

Acknowledgements

I owe an enormous debt of gratitude to those without whom I could not have done this book. To Lauren Johnson, for making me a better writer and reminding me of the joy in book writing. To Sanyika Calloway, for your grace and grit, and joyful friendship. To Melissa Steach, my BFF, and sounding board, you're my ride or die girl for 20+ years and growing. To Toccara Ross, for your get-it-done attitude and slick organization skills. To Adryenn Ashley, for your positivity and sass. For all of the support staff of Bestseller in a Weekend® and The Book Funnel™ including, ghostwriters, editors, book cover designers, website designers, and Marvin Libron, my virtual assistant, I appreciate you.

Mom and dad, you were upset when I didn't include you in the acknowledgements of my first book. I want to make it up to you this time:

I acknowledge you for your love, your commitment, and your no-judgment parenting. Thank you for letting me experience all my "mistakes." Life is messy, and that perspective is priceless. You both gave me the best opportunities, the discipline and the freedom, and you celebrated my inner and outer "wild child." I acknowledge you for never judging and always providing a helping hand; I honor you both and love you with all I am.

To my daughter Isabelle, a.k.a. Izzy Young, who is a daily test of my emotional intelligence meter: you are the gift that keeps on giving, my greatest teacher. I experience a glowing fiery spirit indigo child, rather young woman, in you. You are so tender to those in need. I love you.

To Dietrick, you are my Forest Gump. It's been a wild ride, literally and figuratively. I love doing life with you. To Anthony, thank you for the lessons of unconditional love. To Xena and Jon Bellfield, for your unwavering support and love.

I want to honor all my mentors and coaches, many of them are quoted in this book, including Dr. Mark Goulston, Dr. Betty Uribe, Marla Mattenson, Victor Cheng, Chris Lee, Lewis Howes, Bryan Franklin, Jennifer Russell, Christine Comaford, Michael Ellsberg, Maxine Shapiro and Margo Majdi.

I honor the spirit of God in each and every one of us.

(And if I missed you . . . I'll get you in the next book!)

14729968R00134

Printed in Germany
by Amazon Distribution
GmbH, Leipzig